A HANDMADE MUSEUM

*This book was supported by a grant from
the Greenwall Fund of The Academy of American Poets.*

A HANDMADE MUSEUM

POEMS
BY BRENDA COULTAS

COFFEE HOUSE PRESS

2003

COPYRIGHT © 2003 by Brenda Coultas
AUTHOR PHOTOGRAPH © Bob Gwaltney
COVER AND BOOK DESIGN by Linda Koutsky
PHOTOGRAPHS COPYRIGHT © Brenda Coultas

Coffee House Press books are available to the trade through our primary distributor, Consortium Book Sales & Distribution, cbsd.com or (800) 283-3572. For personal orders, catalogs, or other information, write to: info@coffeehousepress.org.

Coffee House Press is a nonprofit literary publishing house. Support from private foundations, corporate giving programs, government programs, and generous individuals help make the publication of our books possible. We gratefully acknowledge their support in detail on the last page of this book.

LIBRARY OF CONGRESS CIP INFORMATION

Coultas, Brenda.

A handmade museum : poems / by Brenda Coultas. — 1st ed.

p. cm.

ISBN 978-1-56689-143-1 (alk. paper)

I. Bowery (New York, N.Y. : Street) — Poetry. 2. Indiana — Poetry. I. Title

PS3603.O854H36 2003

811'.6—DC21

2003041325

PRINTED IN THE UNITED STATES

ACKNOWLEDGMENTS

Some of these poems were published in *An Anthology of New (American) Poets, Bombay Gin, Conjunctions, Cocodrillo, Double Lucy, Ecopoetics, Epoch, Fence, The Hat, Heights of the Marvelous, Lungfull!, Milk, Psalms 151, Pagan Place, The Poetry Project Newsletter* & web site, *Sycamore Review, Situation, The World,* and *Tool a Magazine.*

Web sites include *Conjunctions, How2,* and the ebook *POeP!* from Rattapallax Press.

A letterpress chapbook *Boy Eye* was published by the Art Institute of Maryland. Sugarbooks published a pamphlet of the farm poems. *A Summer Newsreel* was published by Second Story Press. *The Bowery Project,* along with a critical essay by Alan Gilbert was published by Leroy Press.

The author wishes to thank The Fund for Poetry for giving this writer some time and encouragement.

The author wishes to thank all those, named and unnamed, who listened patiently to this work including Atticus Coultas, Laird Hunt, Robert MacDaniel, Eleni Sikelianos, and Jo Ann Wasserman. Also thank you to members of the writing circle: Marcella Durand, Betsy Fagin, Tonya Foster, Pattie McCarthy, Jeni Olin, Kristin Prevallet, Heather Ramsdell, Diana Ricard, Karen Weiser, and Liz Young. Also thanks to Rembert Block for her assistance with filming "Bowery Box Wishes" and "A Summary of a Public Experiment."

Contents

I

THE BOWERY PROJECT

THE BOWERY PROJECT is centered on the observations of activities that occurred and of objects that appeared on a brief section of the Bowery between Second Street and Houston, an area that contains the remnants of SRO (single room occupancy) hotels and the remains of the 1890s Bowery that are slated to be demolished by The Cooper Square Development Plan in the next year. There are several endangered historic spaces: the artists' co-op (Kate Millett lives there) that used to be McGurk's Suicide Hall (so called because of the numerous suicides by prostitutes that took place there. According to Luc Sante's *Low Life*, in one sample year, 1899, at least six suicides took place), the Sunshine Hotel, and various soup kitchens are on the line. To date, the residents of McGurk's are fighting to preserve their building, which is an important landmark in women's history.

I lived a block from this section and traveled through it daily. My intent was not to romanticize the suffering or demonize the Bowery or its residents, but rather to observe the changes the Bowery was currently undergoing and to write about my own dilemma and identification as a citizen one paycheck away from the street.

The Bowery Project involves experiments in public character as inspired by Jane Jacobs in her landmark attack on urban planning in *The Death and Life of Great American Cities*. Jacobs defines a public character as the person on the street who knows everyone and whom everyone knows; this person serves as the eyes on the street, and thus lends cohesion to the community and serves to prevent crime.

Another book that I took inspiration from was *Sidewalk* by Mitchell Duneier, a five-year study of the lives of black men who sell used books and magazines on Sixth Avenue. Duneier draws upon Jacobs's insight into the use of sidewalks and the role of public characters.

So I began to think about the possibility of leaving the anonymity of the page and becoming a public character, that is, a public poet. The results of two of my experiments in public character are included in THE BOWERY PROJECT

—BRENDA COULTAS, AUGUST 6, 2002

The Bowery Project

AN EXPERIMENT IN PUBLIC CHARACTER

I

The movie star lives in an old furniture store with huge display windows covered with gold blinds. If you look up, you can see the tops of his closets through the 2nd-floor window and you say to yourself with awe, those are the suits of a famous man, those are the wire hangers and sleeves of a famous man.

The Bowery Plan goes something like this: there are explosions and condos arise Las Vegas-like from the smoke. There are floodlights and fireworks or helium balloon races or ribbons cut or ground broken with ceremonial shovels or trees wrapped in yellow ribbons or butterflies, freshly hatched, flying out of boxes. That is the mayor's plan, however mine is different, mine includes groupings of tables and chairs and hanging plants, all portable, public gardens and open houses and a faux suicide reenactment by 5 bungee-jumping squatters at McGurk's Suicide Hall.

Do you remember the stone soup story, how a beggar came to town and began to boil water? Well, bring me a potato. Bring me a story.

I'm not a public character nor do I sleep in open spaces or sleep on bum bed pads in public; rather I sleep and toilet in private and think of public spaces. Inside I eat it all and Sal, our homeless, says he's drinking it all in before heading to Las Vegas. I'll miss our homeless although we don't do anything for him.

Don't like to be touched by ghosts except for invisible ones, not cloudy kinds where you can make out the entire face and hear them speak. Bowery Bum ghosts are real people although they sleep in rooms made of chicken wire. They are not apparitions of McGurk's Suicide Hall or tenement life circa 1900.

I squatted down to touch gray Gap T-shirt on street outside Bowery Bar. I'd just seen an ad of 6 real people wearing same gray T-shirt, thought I could wear this one. Was damp with a liquid, got repulsed, dropped it.

I take a break from the Bowery, on train to Hamptons to see our Joe and Janice. Couple fighting, young man with expensive gangster-rapper pants, hand-tooled 70s belt, two silver mouth studs, perfectly in-your-face Hamptons punk-gangster chic, saying to plain girl, "This is the worst day of my life, you miserable bitch."

Dumpster outside Fisher Sheet Music store.
Can't see into it, must be climbed.

Double-high red dumpster with office debris and a promising office chair, green leather & metal. Circa early industrial 60s, half buried in the rubble. (ASTOR PLACE & LAFAYETTE)

Trash can by Film Anthology; a bright patterned dress pulled out with fingers, label looked expensive, got creeped out, dropped on rim of can, walked on. (2ND ST. & 2ND AVE.)

I have been obsessed with chairs lately. Mostly random chairs and sitting spots, a hidden surprise plastic Adirondack chair by creek, groups of chairs as if in conversation therefore a need for close physical proximity. In restaurants, if you are one person you cannot sit at the 4-top or 6-top; you must sit at the 2-top and they remove the other place setting but leave the chair intact. In photographs of my dad's barn I notice chairs where before I used to notice cats. This time only one cat appears. Up in the hayloft are rockers with missing woven reed seats and a couch that I covered with a sheet against the bird droppings, a great place to sit and look out the window. That is what I do best, sit and look out windows.

Woke up seeing garbage with new eyes and new fresh attitude. Felt transcendental all day.

In order to transform into a public character I need to claim a public space. I will sit in a chair in the Bowery at the same place and time for a season and participate and expedite street life. I'm going to dump it all in, everything that occurs to me or everything I see. That will be my data, my eyes upon the street; the firsthand observation of this last bum-claimed space, a small record before the wrecking ball arrives. I'm taking only pen and notepad. Everything I truly need will appear—I'm not an archaeologist, but am a studier of persons and documenter of trails. (BOWERY & 1ST ST.)

She said he lives here, pointing at the green building, and I said what is he like? "Intense," she said.
I said, thinking about his photographs and how he carves words into his prints, "For a person like that it must be hard to be in the world."
"Yes," she said.
I thought about the emotion of his pictures.
I said, "You can't see inside."
We walked on. (BLEEKER & BOWERY)

I've cultivated a joy of dumpsters out of necessity, romanticized dumpster diving in order to make hunting and gathering interesting. I had a good attitude until recently. I've become ashamed, developed a fear of being yelled at for disturbing the recycling. That's where I get my magazines. Some people say "You love garbage, I've seen you get so excited about it." But really, it's just a glamorous pose.

15

I used to dream of yard sales, where I was the first person there and every collectable I ever desired was on the table, but I had to grab them before the others arrived. I trembled, I tremble in real life before the good stuff.

A Bowery Bum asked "Can I talk to you for a minute?" He burped loudly in my ear. Later he asked me to look up at the sun where he had written his name, then to hug him. I did both. Why do I listen to Bowery Bums?

Peacock fan chair on sidewalk. Another peacock chair lying in vacant lot next to wet, matted rat.

No notable garbage today despite big pile of rubble from the destruction of a collapsed building on 2nd and Houston. Big blue dumpster hauled to the scene. Would I see anything worth recording? Will I have access to that dumpster or will it remain behind the cops' yellow ribbon?

Later remembered sadly that I hadn't thought about my revolutionary idea of surprise chairs in public space. Or the accidental overlooking of sitting space, such as rails without spikes, or bum-friendly stoops like Joe's where Sal lives. This is a new plan, reverse musical chairs. The number of chairs increases every time there's a pause in the honking, holey mufflers, brakes squealing, cell phone conversations, sirens wailing and humans crying. A new chair appears. The point of the game: to seat everyone. The point is that there is a seat for everyone.

II

Orange chair, 70s, metal legs; dirt ring on plastic seat; Apple color printer; metal cig machine on top of dumpster, front opened; air conditioner without a shell. (FEBRUARY 8, 2001, BOWERY & 2ND ST.)

Wooden canvas cot folded up and chairs grouped by a fire hydrant and a man explaining the function of formerly everyday objects because we couldn't understand anymore and we couldn't even see how the body fit into them nor how they could possibly serve it. There was a metal dish on a stand. It was a nurse's basin, he explained. I examined it, turning it over.

There was a long metal cylinder lying on the ground.

"Is that an iron lung?"

"No, that's a midcentury Electrolux."

Puddle of puke. (MARCH 1, 2000, BOWERY & 1ST ST.)

We were talking about the garbage in the 1970s before people got black plastic bags and ruined it. He said you couldn't window-shop big trash night anymore. There was no way to see what was inside the plastic without opening it. He said you should have seen it before, copper pots and pans, designer bric-a-brac, china, crystal, the clothes from Bloomingdale's, no less! All in plain sight. He said imagine the castoffs of the Upper East Side! What glorious days.

Someone said if you had a million dollars I know you'd still work, that's the kind of person you are. What kind of person is that? Then I was very angry at myself for working as if I were a millionaire.

This will be my museum. I'll put it all down here on the page, a portable museum of the 1890s and the 1990s on the Bowery, better'n film, no pocket projectors invented yet, but real words to be copied and read and I write slow cause I expect to live a long time.

What I saw on the Bowery: A bum sitting in an early 20th-century vault, a small vault, front door missing, on its back filled with water and trash and now, a bum drinking out of bag, his ass firmly planted, his arms and legs sticking out. That's what I saw, a resourceful response to chairlessness.

AN EXPERIMENT IN MISERY

"It was late at night, and a fine rain was swirling softly down," wrote Stephen Crane. "That is when I began this experiment in misery." I lived on skid row in Los Angeles in a Bukowski-esque building. I was 20 and a welder by trade, left Firestone Steel, took Greyhound to Los Angeles because in all the articles I had ever read that's where everyone lived. And I had never been much outside the state, knew no one who had been, other than for war.

All the mental hospitals had been emptied out due to a tax cut and there were crazies everywhere or rather more so than usual. On two separate occasions insane persons asked if I had seen her/his identical twin and both showed me a photograph of themselves sans glasses, and said "She/he looks just like me only without glasses." I hung out with an old bum who was a maintenance man at the theater where I worked, who seemed normal but must have gone on long binges where he burned all his bridges. In 1978 I was the elevator operator and wore a bandbox hat and jacket with double rows of brass buttons in a club dedicated to reviving vaudeville. The club's most popular act was the original singer of "Tiptoe through the Tulips," a spunky 80-year-old who played a ukulele.

We went to The Old Pantry restaurant where bums and regular folks lined up to get in, but the bums, who saved up their change all week long, appreciated the bounty the most. Meals were served family style and relish trays of carrot and celery sticks, endless bread, big portions of meat were on every table. There were portraits of the waiters with their years of service listed on the wall. I lived in a studio apartment with a Murphy bed and free roaches. Rent was $125 a month and I was the greenest person ever to live there.

Flowers and graffiti at CBGBS for Joey Ramone. (MAY 1, 2001, BLEEKER & BOWERY)

A tour guide was standing in front, he was saying that it was better to tear down a building than to allow the residents, artists and writers, to live in it paying below market rates. He said that this was his personal opinion and did not represent the views of the Bowery Tour Guide Service.

2 homeless, relaxing inside a cardboard box 20 ft. away. (JUNE 9, 2001, 295 BOWERY)

A church lady rakes through trash for goods, man asleep on sidewalk. (NOON-ISH, JUNE 10, 2001, 1ST ST. & 2ND AVE.)

A lady sitting down in street said, "I like your scarf." Saleswoman said, "I like your shirt." And man walking by said, "That's the second one today." Man on the ground said, "Take me home." Then a man growled and flung a suitcase around in the air. (JUNE 12, 2001)

Two Eames rockers with footstools in a Brooklyn dumpster on Remsen St. I walked by, paused, then walked by again to see if they were really Eameses. A man with white hair said they were original, but no one wanted to pay to have the springs repaired. I climbed to the top, pushed the trash around, trying to decide if they were worth calling home about, heard movement in the bottom, jumped down. I told myself I never really liked Eames rockers. They were uncomfortable, squeaky, and I didn't have room at home for more broken things. (JUNE 15, 2001, BROOKLYN)

The Rat and the Flowerpot

The rat was lying under the window beside shards of my flowerpot and cactus plant on concrete. Some of the shards were on top of the rat. I have some plants on the windowsill one floor up and often find the roots dug up and flower bulbs stolen, thought it was a squirrel. Maybe it was this rat? He was heavy, obese. Maybe he fell and then the pot landed on top? The plant's water dish was still intact on the ledge. Maybe the fall killed the rat? Could a rat climb a brick wall 30 feet up? Why would a rat eat roots with so much fresh garbage on the ground? Could a squirrel have knocked the pot off the ledge just as the rat was walking underneath? What are the odds of the squirrel offing the rat? I couldn't quite put the narrative together. Then I was drunk and still I could not solve the situation. (JUNE 2, 2001, 75 E. 2ND ST.)

New machine on street, red body and silver feed shoot. I studied it. Someone said it was June 8, and the year was 01. (HOUSTON & BOWERY)

WALKING ON THE LOWER EAST SIDE

I'm the life-sized rag doll strapped to my master's shoes dancing salsa in the subway. I'm naked in camouflage paint as a minor detail in a mural of Selena. I'm a brick from the former 5th street squat, I'm a flattened cobblestone you can't see cuz of the trompe l'oeil. Look at me, I'm a white puffy cloud, and now I'm the letters of smoke from a skywriting plane. (FEBRUARY 8, 2001)

Some Public Characters

Old Man Yearby, my grandpa, was a public character in his own grocery store with coal stove, big brass cash register and glass candy case. Inside were bonbons, horehound candy shaped like bacon strips, stick candy in a jar. He spent afternoons in a lawn chair by the meat case, cutting bologna, making onion salad in a cup, and swatting flies. His dog was public too. Minnie Yearby wore glasses, sat upright, smoked cigars, and made change.

My whole tribe/nation of my mother's side, my grandpa and uncles were all public (politicians) characters. They named our village after us, Yearbyville. You could just say your name and "put it on credit." You could just say, "I'm a Yearby," and be on your way.

Then my parents had a country store, the Midway Market, and we went by my father's name. We were the public Coultases living in full view of the school bus, doing homework and drinking pop in lawn chairs in our place of business.

I thought marriage would be my most public act and performance or my baptism or once when I had taken an oath to defend the public or when I was a Girl Scout pledging to do my best to honor God and my country, and once when I was in the newspaper because I was a welder and a fashion model, and then I got stalked, and once when they used to call me Puffy Coultas.

Bum Stash: Early 21st Century

The lot had been emptied by the police/city who put up a new fence and padlock, took down the trees and crops, and replaced soil with gravel. This year some crops pushed up again. Objects returned, this time under plastic, a long, low stick of furniture with nine drawers, one missing, a yellow mustard color. Someone built a lean-to from mattresses, not steady, and positioned a hubcap to shelter a plant from sun. Someone collected the brass number 5, strung it on a wire, and someone added a brown chipped water pitcher.

Later observed in secret, a man with magenta hair, adding objects he found on the street. I saw him sitting on a broken rowing machine and then on a broken stationary bike; the exercise equipment rested on the gravel. When he left he locked the gate with his own working lock.

Bum stash tore apart. Lean-to pushed over, same objects, but did the police or the magenta man tear it all down? (MAY 15, 2001)

Lot cleared and new gravel laid down, an orange shopping cart chained to fence. (MAY 25, 2001)

Orange shopping cart unchained and rolled to street corner, miniature boxed pie and particle board inside basket. (JUNE 10, 2001, IST ST. & 2ND AVE.)

Two white 70s appliances/On one corner, washer with an oval window in the door, laundry inside w/brown mold/on the other corner, dryer./No one can write much nowadays because it takes money/in the 70s people wrote all the time/now we don't have room to lay it all out, so lay parts at a time, pick them up and then lay some more/I iron and bake that way and try to think of things to do for money/crochet and knit/sell blood and hair/pick garbage for copper and aluminum. When my husband left, I thought I could start to lay it out, move it around, until an alchemy took hold. /So I laid it all out: 2 super 8s, a 35 mm, found photos, books of the Bowery, poetry, and there was lots of poetry./Artifacts, flattened bottle caps, rusted cans, early tin cans, many interesting screws and bolts, sometimes found machines in enamel green, and sometimes bobbins and thread./I laid it all out/stared at it/moved it/talked to myself about it/read it all again/waited/nothing happened./I put it all back. (APRIL 27, 2001, 75 E. 2ND ST.)

BOWERY MIND

He said it too (a man in a book about the chicken wire hotels), a mantra I had
been saying all along in my head:
When they tear down the Bowery
When they implode the Bowery
When they blow up the Bowery
When they demolish the Bowery
When they revise the Bowery
When they renovate the Bowery
When they rehabilitate the Bowery

He said they suffered from Bowery Mind; the residents never expected to
spend the remainder of their lives in single rooms, each taken up by a long, nar-
row bed and hot plate. I said to my husband, "We'll live in this apt., these 4
rooms for the rest of our lives. This is where we will grow old together. We will
never be able to live anywhere else. We'll never have the money or the time to
find another place." At first it made me cry and then later it became very satis-
fying to say, "This is the bed, the room, the place I will die in." It settles the
mind. People think it's tragic to be old in New York City, but maybe it's just
tragic to be old anyplace.

Once people moved away from farms and came to cities, all saying this is what
I did, this is what I did for posterity. Along came me saying this is what I did
for poetry. A lot of people came here all at once, this is how and why my tene-
ment exists.

A man lying in a prone position on sidewalk outside vacant lot. The lot was covered in white poison. The pile of bottles had been getting tall. I could imagine a bottle village or other folk shrine (even the Mennonites in Illinois had a building made of Fresca bottles), the glass was rising to the top of the chain links like a transparent pool without swimmers. (AFTERNOON, MAY 8, 2001, BOWERY & IST ST.)

He said he was once the most powerful drug dealer on the block and, "go fuck yourself." I saw him later, carrying around a strange sculpture difficult to describe, because there was no comparison to it in the natural world. (2ND ST. & 2ND AVE.)

Man carrying a deflated blow-up doll in basket, said he would wash it and hang it on the wall to make a statement, collecting graffiti tags, said he's going to make a coffee table book. In bodega, man said with body language "give me 3 numbers, and I'll give you 3" in reference to lotto. We both lost the 33 million. (HOUSTON & ALLEN)

Man with huge, flopping boil on neck. His hands were empty. (EARLY MORNING, APRIL 29, 2001, BLEEKER & BOWERY)

A man carrying a cross and a cane, wearing headphones. (APRIL 28, 2001, WHITE HOUSE HOTEL)

Some Might Say That All I've Done Is Stack Up a Heap of Objects

Some will say it's all been done before, and that others have done better but still I stack things up. I don't think about it, I put blinders on but hope that through accumulation they'll form a pattern out of chaos. I've stacked up twigs one by one, building a structure, weaving and shaping, forming a skeleton out of raw garbage transformed into beauty, maybe with something to say to any Bowery resident or reader of poetry. Please, I am intentionally writing this for you.

Glass Beach

Tide was in and so looked at tree line of the landfill, could see bottles entwined in the roots, glass shards, and garbage compressed to a great density so as to become brown matter. I could see whole bottles that would be free in time and pulled one out, it had a brown liquid in it. Became entranced, curious if this was the original content. Or was it just rot and sea water? A newspaper from the 1940s was lying on some wood, intact except for the edges; in fact, so fresh one could easily turn the pages. I wondered if someone had wedged it out from the roots or had the waves worked it free? Some person who cared about such things as history had placed it there. In fact, there were other scavengers who worked the beach silently setting aside vintage pop bottles and curiosities in a safe place for others like us.

We spoke to a man scratching the sand with a stick looking for marbles. He knew the history of this place, said it was a horse-rendering plant and indeed on the map it said Dead Horse Bay, and it had been a city dump that became a town composed of the dump's employees, then the city closed it down stating it was too toxic to live in. Now it was an unmarked stretch of public beach that the residents returned to regularly and bitterly.

The old glass had a lot of lead and it gleamed. I tried not to be greedy and to take only what I could carry. Meanwhile I left thousands. The broken glass tinkled in the surf and if I ever were to believe in mermaids, this is where they'd be. (JULY 24, 2001)

Later, picked up 2 toy guns, ink well, sm brw, sm brw, 2 wh cold creams. Went home. (JULY 27, 2001, GLASS BEACH, BROOKLYN)

29

Later

Thought I'd never "look like money." (AUGUST 1, 2001)

Looked in regular spot, nothing. (APRIL 27, 2001)

Went to Coney Island with some poets. We had a good time although the garbage was unremarkable. (MAY 5, 2001)

70s fake Victorian settee with toaster oven and orange juicer in original box. (AUGUST 30, 2001, 2ND ST. & 2ND AVE.)

Four panels of fake bookcases, 2 tabletops, glass chandelier, slightly broken, and man, with a cart painted blue and decorated with glamorous dolls, sizing it up. We stopped to discuss the objects. We guessed at their origin, maybe from the vaudeville days of a famous Bowery theater and shook our heads in shame that we couldn't take any of it with us although it was cool stuff. (LABOR DAY WEEK-END, 1ST & BOWERY)

Shopping cart painted red, metal 70s office chair. Man put small table in trash can and walked away. (SEPTEMBER 4, 2001, HOUSTON & ELIZABETH)

After the 11th

Were they ever visible from this street? Does it matter if I say they were visible from Houston & Bowery if they weren't? But most certainly they were. How little attention I pay to things outside my personal space, never had a reason to think about them, only used to wonder why I never took anyone there, and had meant to but was scared of them.

Thought it would come out in the writings like dreams or nightmares, it would manifest and that writing it all down was important if just to say here's a document very pretty and well-written, read about our reactions and grief.

In my city were people and no ark to save them, just arms to carry them in. To say that I loved a city, a deeply flawed one, but to know that I did and that my life might end because I couldn't abandon her now. And if ever I would leave, it would be for nature. Nature would have to make up for what I'd lose in culture. Although there is nature in this city: tamed chunks of wood nearly identical tied up in string into a tidy bundle or slender slices of wood gently laid down by trash can and wrapped in some cord or string of various textures and sadly, big bustling log beams in dumpsters to be hauled away. But some of it is wild, there are morning glories thickly growing on the chain link fences, locust trees growing out of rock, still human nature is what the city grows best. There are peddlers laying out books in rows on sidewalk or tabletop, very good ones, and shoes lined up by size and color. One peddler ran after us saying "I will not be undersold." The merchandise pulled out of garbage, reasonably clean, ready to wear, and ready-to-read very good books.

Man in turban wearing pin, reads, "I'm a Sikh, God bless America."

Elbow pipe, wood stacked and tied in bundles, 2 couches across the street from one another. (OCTOBER 18, 2001, 1ST ST. & 2ND AVE.)

One evening there appeared 7 dusty theater seats circa 1900, with a fleur-de-lis on one side. They were bolted to a piece of flooring, the backs were crimson velvet, and the leather seat cushions laid on the sidewalk. The chairs stayed for 3 days and were soon joined by an 80s office chair broken into parts.

I had seen a web site of haunted photographs, with ectoplasm and orbs and wondered what ghosts inhabited these chairs, what old Bowery asses once sat there.

Later in same spot gold baroque chair, gone right away. (NOVEMBER 12, 2001)

Getting cooler at night, thought of how cold the workers' hands will get. How cold until they suspend the dig. (OCTOBER 25, 2001)

Mail cart with 2 face masks dangling from handle. (NOVEMBER 2, 2001)

Two matching sofas with TV resting on seat. A day later, TV on sidewalk between them and only the wooden skeletons of couches remain. (OCTOBER 30, 2001, 1ST ST. & 2ND AVE.)

Later man with bed roll sleeping by wooden skeletons and then two days later, a man sleeping inside them with his shopping cart beside him, TV, screen cracked on ground. Shell removed. (NOVEMBER 8, 2001)

Golden legless couch, early American style, 60s, where cushions used to be, the newspaper with a color photograph of the president and a flag. (NOVEMBER 7, 2001)

Tenement Tour

I wanted everyone to see how we lived and I had my own questions. Were we identical to other husbands and wives, to the other couples stacked above and beside us? Like Joe and Janice across the street or the wealthy European next door? I had been making a great effort to be like everyone else lately or else to be invisible. I couldn't afford new clothes and a dead rat lay in front of my winter clothes stored in the basement. So until I decided to face the rat, slide the dustpan under him and carry him away, I would be invisible.

Had to tell the tourists that tenement life was much better these days, we were nearly middle class and that only 2 people lived in these 4 rooms. That poor people couldn't live in them anymore, no immigrants like in Jacob Reis or Herbert Ashbury's time. Tenements are now expensive and the truly poor live in a worse kind of projects or in Queens while hobos and bums live in Rockaway Beach. We could barely afford this tenement life. We were not moving up socially or economically nor were we ambitious that way. We wanted to retreat or at least maintain the status quo until one day when we might have more than rent money . . . then there would be woods, cabin or cottage.

So wrote script, recorded it, and customers listened as they toured each room.

Bowery Box Wishes

FILM SCRIPT FOR A HOME MOVIE: 3 MINS, B & W

PROPS: A silver foil-covered or battered "Lottery" style box labeled "Bowery Wishes" mounted on street furniture or maybe wired to a chain link fence.

DIRECTIONS: Film opens at 1st & Bowery. Film hands writing down wishes and then hands folding the paper into shapes, paper airplanes, or elaborate angles then placing wishes in box. Also provide found stationery, as odd as possible. Film various hands, however they appear: some in gloves or with elaborately painted nails, or natural hands of various individuals. Some tramps, some yuppies, and some poets. Do not film faces.

OBSERVATION NOTES: Some began by clearing their throats and minds, by sitting down, selecting a pen, selecting paper in the color or in the best shape of their wishes. One wrote a very long wish written over a long time, but mostly the wishes were on the tip-top of their thoughts, not buried or deeply buried but near the top, accessible. Many held the pen tightly, many wore bracelets. Some were black and some were white, both men and women. Some came from the mission where there was a hot food line so many of the wishers and dreamers came over. One man, his glasses held on by string, promised he'd bring more people over and he was good to his word. Some wrote as if I had the ability to make the wishes come true. A man in a Three Stooges shirt said he had lived on the Bowery all his life, and he was looking for a girlfriend. Another said he had just yesterday gotten out of jail, and he was a poet, and then he recited a poem. Some women stopped, they were silent and diligent about their wishing. They did not say if they were lonely what they were looking for.

Then it was over and I had a box of wishes.

"Are you going to read them?" someone asked.
"No," I said. But I wasn't sure why, I had promised them nothing yet I felt
that they had trusted me not to look, but maybe some of them hoped to be
heard. Months later, I took the box down and realized that what I felt was the
need to protect them. So I did.

Things I Found December 15, 2001

MORNING

Apartment sale notice, tore off pole and put in purse in case I went in that direction. Spools of waxed leather-like string on 2nd Street. Earlier there were more, but I forgot about them, meaning to pick them up on my way home, but instead went a different direction, so went back later, only two spools left. Black and tan. Further east, a metal chair, brown, facedown, and folded.

EVENING

From a box of books on 1st Street *In the Summer House*, Jane Bowles, 1954. An old nervous man on his way to the Catholic Worker for dinner said he collected books of airships, and were there any books on airships in the box? He said things were harder for people like himself since Sept. 11th, but thought new mayor might be good. We shook hands and I couldn't think of the right words to reassure him with.

NIGHT

Then there were the things I wished I'd found: A Bowery flophouse at $10 a night; Stephen Crane; a rainbow; my grandpa's trick dog Minnie, long gone; Rusty, Dad's old dog; my pig Dogfood and my pony Soybean Saint. Wish I'd found my grandpa strolling the street, my grandmas and my dad. It was the dead I wished I could find on this mythological stretch of skid row. Oh, that and a tin of marbles.

Parking lots cleared out by city, a 2-wheel plastic cart, big, on its side, garbage, not trash in the bitter cold. Returning by car, saw long abandoned grocery cooler, like from our old store, the Midway Market. Cold out. (DECEMBER 31, 2001, HOUSTON & BOWERY)

Sightings

Something brown, square, and made of fabric, can't remember what it was: clothes on hangers as if for sale and hanging on gate in snow, tilted firescape held up with rope, mail cart with bucket inside, lump under cover next to shopping cart chained up. (395 BOWERY)

One covered with bright blue top. Fridge w/o door, new graffiti. Office chair on wheels, plastic, blue upholstery could be dried out and recovered, I thought, all isn't lost on this chair.

Green locker, single size but what era? Seems very old judging by dirt. Flimsy dresser missing handles but with all the drawers, a fake wood desk depressing and ugly. Big red dumpster with blue mattress on top. Some protest signs in Spanish, calling for revolution, newspaper with a shit smear. (MARCH 19, 2002)

Someone said now that you're married, you can't bring all that stuff home anymore. Yes, this was true, so I photograph it or commit it to memory.

In movies and other parts of the country I have seen that people live in houses with functioning refrigerators and stoves and that they have closets, basements, yards, barns, and attics, that people have space for both new and old things. For example, my mother has 6 riding mowers, of which two work part of the time. Some of the mowers are from the 70s and I rode them as a teenager, and how excited we were at this new prospect in lawn management. The mowers rest permanently in the shade beneath a tree because the barn is stuffed with numerous push mowers. I thought maybe she should get rid of some of the mowers, but now they are collector's items like my dad's crank-up tractor with metal wheels. And now she has 30 years invested at no cost. Although none of them are complete in themselves maybe the others could be cannibalized into a whole working model. Not to sidetrack, but this is what I hear about what goes on in other parts of the country. That people, if they really want, can have (keep) it all.

At the End of the Month
in the Beginning of the Year

I

We stopped to consider a wooden rickety chifforobe that needed some nails. Getting it in, he broke my favorite vase, bent my best lamp, and chipped our only piece of new furniture, a wardrobe made of pressed wood chips and covered in fake, wood-like paper. Later, a dresser upside down, the workers emptying out the apt. asked me if I wanted it. I had no husband with me, so went home alone and empty-handed, and there went all that real wood into the dumpster. (JANUARY 27, 2002, BOWERY & 1ST)

In the 1980s (Reagan years), I used to have vast collections and my rent was $200 a month. I had reams of fabrics, buttons and bric-a-brac from auctions and thrift shops. I only wore clothes from the 40s, down to my shoes, and I wore a lot of gaberdine men's shirts which mostly cost $1 each. So I bought them all, and in this way I was fashionable. Sometimes I drove a hundred miles to Louisville, Kentucky to eat lunch and to shop at a place that billed itself as the world's largest thrift store.

Every Saturday was the St. Vincent 10-cent sale. At daybreak, cardboard boxes of clothes were forklifted to the parking lot. We waited behind a gate until the bell went off, then we ran in, grabbing and seizing everything shiny, bright, or sequined.

II

Things given back to street: green sweater (pulled from trash and dry-cleaned), found basket (torn handle). (FEBRUARY 2, 2002)

A futon mattress, the frame torn into smaller pieces, brown felt western hat. (FEBRUARY 23, 2002, BOWERY & HOUSTON)

Ice cream or frosty drinkmaker machine on its back. I stopped to examine it and to help a man who was lifting a wheelchair up and over a 6-ft high fence. He shook my hand. Bought 8 T-shirts that said something about New York, that I loved it or that I had seen Little Italy or Chinatown or Spider-Man, bought Gucci watch, $10, on Canal St. (JUNE 15, 2002, LOWER EAST SIDE)

RETURN TO GLASS BEACH

The soles of shoes appear first, some pointing in that direction. The hidden stand where the bumper sticker man usually rests. Maybe we should look at it closely now because when he returns in the summer we won't be able to. I found a section of ceramic blue birds like from a cuckoo clock, picked it up and carried it around, a child's white teacup with missing handle, left them there on a wooden beam. Stared at objects ensnared in a ball of tree roots, got down close trying to decipher this knot of stuff, but didn't try to remove any of it. Everything from the summer was still there; the ceramic light sockets, license plates, and the wooden hull on which to pass on things to others. However, the garbage did not excite; instead, it depressed me. (FEBRUARY 2002, BROOKLYN)

Application

Found myself locked in Bowery mindset, settling for less, or the reality, that my dreams were just fantasies of success and that I didn't have the appropriate language for making things happen. The application asked me what would I do with the money, so I was trying to write a paragraph about what I would use free money for. "To buy time" I wrote, "and a new camera," but there was more space, so "I might buy a new tablecloth and paint, I've been wanting to redecorate for a while or I might go to Gettysburg with the money, everyone says it's worth seeing. I might buy yoga lessons, and I'd like to take a gourmet cooking or a photography class, also get some pictures framed and a headstone for dad and get mom's cats neutered."

I wanted to buy a block of time thinking of a salt block, of how long it took the cows to lick it down into a strange shape, and once I licked the block myself, but can't remember the taste or later, the taste of the cows, even the ones I'd named. I couldn't explain that although my project was inexpensive it was actually priceless, or that I would do it anyway, with or without the money. Maybe slower or with more stress. Some things wouldn't get done, the things that took cash, not time. Or maybe I would give up altogether, which was something I thought about regularly. I wasn't sure what they wanted to hear. Since I didn't know, I became nervous. The free money had been won by many people who live on my block, and I thought if I could find the right speech the money would then be mine. (APRIL 14, 2002, 75 E. 2ND ST.)

Revelation

The landlord pulled a dumpster up to our door, and into it went the contents of the basement. There were things of my own I had to retrieve and, having no place for them, out onto the street they went. Mostly I gave up books, one called *I Love Adventure* with a zebra-striped cover, a Warhol catalog; a leather suitcase, maybe rhino skin, circa 1940, beaten and busted up but of such exotic character that I had held onto it for 5 years. It was odd that I wasn't interested in our very own dumpster even though it was full of good things. Right away I saw a man rooting around and carting off a dusty garish print with a garish gold frame. Some punk girls were on top and very happily shouting "teeth." In the center of the dumpster were hundreds of white boxes, that I thought were empty gift boxes from a craft project or something. Instead they were filled teeth impressions from the 70s, whole uppers and lowers set in mostly yellow clay-like material, plus some single teeth, ivory colored, and possibly real.

A woman with a baby carriage stopped to comment on the wonder of it. My friend called her sister so she could come down and take a look. One man, an artist, came back twice and said he could do a study of the dentistry of Eastern-European immigrants, that's whose impressions these were. Inside the hallway the landlord had set aside a box for himself.

Passing by later while it was still light, I saw that someone had lined up a row on the dumpster ledge. Gnarly, that's the best word to describe this forest of teeth and the roofs of thousands of mouths. Amazing. How primitive teeth are, right up there with alligators.

Still, I was not excited for myself, but I was happy for everyone else, and when people walked by I said "teeth" too. I knew it would make them happy to see a dumpster full of them. I thought about my lack of excitement, I never even kept a pair, only photographed a couple, and all this time, for years, I was literally sitting one floor above the mother lode, the site of a chapter into the history of dentistry, and I was not excited. I thought about it for a week.

I realized that the garbage had lost its appeal because I no longer had room. Our bedroom was filled with mismatched crippled furniture, some missing just a leg and propped up with a book or newspaper. A collection of lamps each with its own distinct dysfunction; one shaped like a Chinese junk that worked for a whole month and could never be coaxed to light up again. But I had bought it for my husband's birthday, so it was a keeper. Plus, I had gotten some clothes from my cousin, and I had books to read. Thus I was filled up and overflowing with things. Maybe garbage would never again be interesting to me. I hoped that I would get my enthusiasm back because there is, after all, a shitload in this world. (MAY 3, 2002, 75 E. 2ND ST.)

Gumball

Aquamarine dumpster named Gumball, outside window, empty. Men from across the street filled it all day long. An eager man stood by taking what he could, he left an old model boat that was missing the sail. He took a small desk instead because he could sell it. He said they were cheapos, that the contractor and workers were destroying the furniture before it hit the street. He said if it were his job he'd put the furniture out, let people take it and then the dumpster would hold more. He had a great plan for how the dumpster should be filled, for he had studied on it. By day's end, Gumball was brimming, overflowing, and surrounded by the homeless. (APRIL 11, 2002, 75 E. 2ND ST.)

CONSTRUCTION

Through the cutout a bulldozer travels back and forth, leveling the earth. Across the street, a monster crane raises dorm walls up to the air. Whole walls and windows soar into sky, then are dropped into human hands and set in place.

The iron pillars went in during February and I had hoped to ignore the whole thing.

What had been an empty lot, then a plant nursery, is now a building site for NYU dorms. Across the street another one is going up. I'm not sure what it's to be. Old Capital Silver, a restaurant supply house, is being remodeled, so at least the building is saved. The night they emptied it, we were going to a reading and saw the big dumpster. Graciously they had left out a small oak desk, we considered it (needing a desk), but it was dry rotted and the wood came away in our hands. By the time we returned, there was a man on top pulling out what he could, and it was dark. (APRIL 21, 2002, 2ND ST. & BOWERY)

A Summary of a Public Experiment

One day I gathered up a table and a chair and put up a sign that read, "Tell me a Bowery story." My friend came with a video camera. Some people wanted to know if we could make them famous, some wanted to know if their parents would see them. Some were performers and trying to give me what they thought I wanted.

He had returned from the South, to try his luck again in New York City. He did not want to go back, because of the Confederate flag. He was a large homeless fellow, middle-aged, he began with the 70s and how there were 5 blocks of bars and bodies lying side by side, end to end, and onto the 80s crack epidemic into the 90s gentrification. He showed me his bus ticket, asked for some spare change and spoke a long time as if to earn it.

One sat down and told us his name, and that he was a resident of the Bowery area, from Houston Street to Cooper Union Square. He said that he grew up in Brooklyn, on the streets as a member of the Young Skulls gang. He said, "Things changed for me here. This is where it changed at, there's a lot of resources around here, for anybody that's on the street. Some people are so accustomed to bathhouses, soup kitchens. That's all they know, they don't feel safe inside a city shelter . . . they kinda feel safer in the street, on the sidewalk or in the park. They are woken up in the morning by police at 5:30. By the time people are going to work, they don't see us. . . . I have a gratitude for the Bowery, it's the only place I feel at peace."

A young man and an older man with a stoma stopped. The older one talked through a microphone that he pressed up against his larynx. Still it was hard to make out the words. He was dapper, very slim, and he thought himself well-preserved, but he did not wish to appear on camera. The younger one told us that he grew up here, that his pop had a plumbing shop for 25 years. He became friends with some underground people from across the street, some Yippies, one of them fixed his minibike. One day he came home and saw people standing around and the Yippie's dad looking sad. The Yippie had taken some LSD, was coming down Bleeker, and imagined the police were after him and took off on the minibike so fast that he hit a lamppost, flew up and hit the wall of a building on Broadway and Bleeker. A month later, the old man (the father) was found in his room, dead of an overdose. "His son was his whole life, Poor soul . . . broken, laid him to rest the best we could. I liked him so much."

"This was before co-opville," he said, "You can't even live now in the Bowery for god's sake. Bums slice someone's face for a cigarette . . . A WWI vet lost his legs, not in the service but on a train, Pops got him a lawyer, got to the Empire State Building, F. Lee Bailey. Got $100,000. . . . His cut was $30,000. Got a brand new van, would write my brother a check every day for a fifth of Fleischmann's . . . drank it nonstop, literally drank himself to death. He was a good person, god bless his heart. Gotta stop talking about the old days, make myself really sad. Bums sliced someone up for a drink of wine, on check days it was a nightmare. Wasn't like they were always down on their luck, like the great depression, it was dangerous. Someone robbed a church, they took the chalice. We're Jewish, but my father paid the thief $100. He said 'I respect people's religion, I don't believe in that cops stuff. You do something wrong like that I don't go for that.' The church was so grateful, . . . The 70s, what a sorry time that was."

Another man said, "I seen a lot of things and I heard a lot of things but most of all the Bowery is a nice place to live. People shop and give money to poor people. The Caucasian people are very courteous towards the Negro person. And um, I'm trying to get a place elsewhere. And um, I have a lot of assistance from the Caucasian people. I don't see anything wrong with the things going on. That's what I have to say."

A man walking with a cane said, "Might see anything anytime. I've seen so much I can't explain." We asked him if he could tell us just one thing that he saw on the Bowery, but he would not sit down and he would not explain.

This one didn't think he was handsome anymore and so did not want to be on camera. He remembered the bodies on the street. Another man walked by, turned around and stated, "There's a carnival going on down the street." Another said he couldn't think of a story. He said, "You know what I used to love? It was on television, *The Bowery Boys* with Alec Guiness, that was about 1954."

A man came by who got out of the Bowery. He was a migrant from North Carolina, he couldn't cash a check, the only money he had, so he camped out in front of the mission with a group of other men for 30 days and he had 3 hot meals a day there. He got out, he said, because he was on a different mission.

Only one woman stopped, she was smoking a cigarette and holding a blue shopping bag. She was very pretty but looked too young to have a Bowery story but she did. She had been in NYC for 10 years off and on, bartending with acting on the side, her rent was originally $251. Now she was okay but not where she felt she should be. She had stayed in a lot of flophouses with her boyfriend. She said, "If you stay in that kind of place . . . rip the bedspread off. It might have bedbugs. I feel okay with the sheets, they bleach them, and never never ever touch the bed itself."

A teen with a green mohawk and his mother making a pilgrimage to CBGBS walked by, but they would not tell me a story.

Three male teenagers on their way to a pot parade who said "We like to get high, we get high every day," stopped. They were very high, but really they did not have a story. They had not lived long enough or in the right time to have a Bowery tale.

A poet came over and told us the first thing he did when he arrived was to take a suit that his father had given him and sell it to the rag trade there. The

Bowery was full of used men's clothing stores and filled with bums. He said Bowery and Houston was the Times Square of downtown, he shot a video and did a play there. He knew a poet who hung out at the Mars Bar who would look out and say, "There's the street of lost souls." He never thought "bum" was a derogatory term. He even met a poet from Luxembourg who said, "When we get old let's be Bowery Bums, Bowery Bums." He pointed to an alley and said there will be 700 apartments there in 3 years. He said there would be a promenade here. He said, "We'll sit down to play checkers and buy flowers." He pointed out the buildings that were saved and those that were going down. He had watched The Whitehouse Hotel turn from flophouse to a Eurotrash hostel. He believes that the Bowery will always have an edge, because it's theatrical. He always thinks of E. E. Cummings's poem about the Third Avenue El, that Cummings said that when the El was torn down, the u.s. sold the steel to Japan and that it came back to us as bullets.

Bowery Hank said he could tell us everything we needed to know. He said that this was not skid row but a working class neighborhood. That very few people were bums, that out of two-three thousand men "there were 6 drunks on the floor so everybody was bums." He said, "I'll show you how crazy the Bowery is, in 1957 I had holes in my shoes, in 1958 I owned two bars and a white Cadillac . . . Very good to me, very trustworthy . . . people didn't understand why I loved the Bowery. Number 1, I made a lot of money. Number 2, I got shot twice and got stabbed numerous times but that has nothing to do with it when you're on the battlefront. . . . Every day was a new adventure, I catered to a lot of people who were very prominent in show business: Truman Capote, Judy Garland, Lee Marvin. Owned 6 bars, I was a young guy and if you had problems in your bar we would stay for a month until you didn't have any more problems."

"This man couldn't say Hank, he said 'Zank.' He was a refugee from the war. He said 'Zankie, take the bar, take the bar, I can't take it no more.' 'I ain't got 12 cents.' I told him. He said 'You owe me ten thousand.' . . . I took the key and threw it away, and I said to myself I'm never going to lock the bar until I get it paid off. I brought my ladies in, I had a shower and a bed in the back, I didn't leave for one year, I paid that man off. . . . It was a great life. . . . This is bullshit, these bars, these clubs, 'Hi, how are you?' Who cares? Do you think I'd talk to those people, never in a million years. Bowery, Bowery Bums, you hear that shit, but the Bowery was different. Men worked. They were coal heavers, cowpunchers, seamen. Did you know there was a cow farm in Brooklyn on Pritken Avenue? . . . They were never bums in my eyes. There were coal shovelers from Ireland, big shovels like this (gestures with hands), . . . No one knows about that," he said. "I'm the Bowery man."

My own tale is of walking and observing, of imagining. I was not a homeless or passed out on the sidewalk, but maybe I was drunk on the Bowery once. I must have been drunk or tipsy or hungover or sweating or tired there or once happy there too. I was in a good mood or optimistic about the future and I must have enjoyed the sights and smells (of which reminds me of the county fair the day our hog pit filled with good slop, that ripe smell of grease and sweat). I must have been drunk and fallen asleep and must have gotten a blanket or newspaper out of the trash and must have found a box and curled up in it and I must have built a shelter just for one night, must have been tired and not able to imagine how to get home. Maybe my feet hurt. I might have been sick. I might have been a backslider, or I could have been tempted by an abandoned couch, and laid down for a nap. I must have made a home for the night and I must have been scared but soon dozed off despite the fear and discomfort and I must have hid my face from people, which is what I do when I feel ugly or unhappy and I must have been ashamed and so although all this time I was living in full view of the public, nobody saw me.

NOTE: In editing I followed Allen Ginsberg's advice "to notice what's vivid." I tried to be as accurate as possible, and to capture the essence of what people said about Bowery life. I also edited for clarity, coherence, and economy.

II

An American Movie

"It's all right, it's okay. There's something to live for. Jesus told me so."
—Uncle Bill, *from* American Movie (*draw out*)

Scene i

This eye opens on Houston and Avenue A, on a mural of Princess Di, it reads:
"We fought for 200 years to throw off the yoke of British oppression. Die Di."

The eye moves to Avenue A and 14th, mural of Princess Di and Mother
Theresa, side by side.

Repeat after me:
"In Memory of Royalty and Holiness,
Audience repeats
Rest in Peace"
Audience repeats

I met a man the week of back-to-back funerals whom I later married. We
watched both.

In the church was a basket full of prayers.
I read them.
What were people praying about, and were their prayers any different than mine?

I visit the stations of the cross
I have felt the power of prayer before.
This is written as one who's gotten good at prayer.

I put my own in.

"Signed SWALCAKWS (sealed with a lick cuz a kiss won't stick),
Brenda"

I move my lips do you?
I wonder if I'm doing it right?
I say it in my head. Like this,

Dear God,
Please watch over us and please watch over my brother and my sisters and
mom and dad
please watch over those in need
in Jesus' name we pray,
Amen.

I say this every night.
Is it too dull to reach the universe?

Dear Universe,
Why do you hear the Mayor's prayers and not mine?

Yours, Brenda

Dear Universe,
You must be a male

you are not unisex

you are just fashionably androgynous.

Sorry to bug you, Brenda

I write poems for the public.

I call myself Brenda Coultas.

I write public poems.

I write poems for twenty, that's twenty people to a poem.

A man sells poems in the subway,

Published Poet is his name.

It costs whatever you want to give him.

I'm the same, it's whatever you want to give me only I want everything.

He paints portraits of "retired" Beanie Babies:

Digger the Crab

Doby the Doberman

Doodle the Rooster

Dotty the Dalmatian

Ears the Rabbit

Fetch the Retriever

Flash the Dolphin

Fleece the Lamb

Flip the Cat

Floppity the Bunny

Freckles the Leopard

Garcia the Ty-Dye Bear

Glory the Bear

Goldie the Fish

Gracie the Swan

Grunt the Razorback

Happy the Hippo

Hippity the bunny

Hoot the Owl

Inch the Inchworm

Inky the Pink Octopus

Scene 3

Hi, I am a word that exists on the soles of your shoes.
Please stop walking on me.

Hi, I am a royal Fergie mug.
I was chubby and engaged.
Now I'm skinny, divorced, chipped, and stained.

Hi, I am a Cabbage Patch doll
preserved in the attic in my original wrapper.
I am so ugly I am cute. I look and feel like a fetus with an engorged head.

Hi, I am an adorable discontinued Beanie Baby.
I am the rarest Beanie Baby of them all.
Collectors will commit crimes in order to possess me.
I fit in the hand like a small living dog.

Hello, I am a Pee-Wee Herman doll
I have a soft body and a hard plastic head.
I know what I am but what are you?

INSIDE THE WEATHER
AN INTERPRETATION OF 16 MM EDUCATIONAL FILM
Inside the Weather
DUMPSTER DIVING ON 2ND ST. & AVE. A, MAY 9, 2000

I don't have a 16 MM projector so I'll read it this way (by hand)
Take it apart put it back together again
I take it out and I put it back. Forward and reverse
There's a thin spot where the real world shines through
A thin spot in thinning places from going back and forth.

This is some sort of silent reading
Weather is sometimes quiet and creepy-crawls Manson family-like.

It's raining outside, I go back to unreeling: A shot of an airplane. Passengers
buckle up, the captain greets them. Plane taxis (shots of the plane and its belly).
Passengers looking out window enjoying marvelous weather. A planet appears in
center of frame, then a thousand frames of a curved cylinder maybe an engine.
A strip of sound on the side. Can't hear it through fingers (film breaks).

The weather is a Bowery bum penis tip urinating on a trash can.
Jars of penis tips like Planters roasted nuts
I enjoy formerly living things in lab jars
Mr. Peanut walks down the Bowery, you can smell his roasted nuts

Touched by tip of Bowery bum penis, tried not to look, just felt tip touch lightly
on neck
Touching cocks back and forth on the tips.

I take them out and put them back

Holding film up to 100-watt bulb, burn eyeballs. Looking at the plane in the waves of the sky. More earth and now night. Could they be circling the globe? Could they no longer be earth citizens, rather citizens of the air?

(Unspool reel with pencil in center) Smell of film chemicals is nothing like the smell of clouds or the sun or rain or hail. The smell is vinegary like a hundred dirty socks on the feet of fifty Bowery bums.

Once I was in the sky thinking about the people in the film about weather. Once I was in an airplane too, smiling and pointing like happy people in a film about the joys of weather.

My lips crackle. Turn on www.raincam.com. The voice spoke through a tiny transistor radio. A blue and silver transistor radio in its original box, the top eaten off by rats. It said loudspeaker-like "People of the Bowery, take shelter now."

A school of blind albino fish swim inside an underground lake in Mammoth Cave. They say "It's all about the weather this season."

This is tedious work, and rereeling is tuff   film twists like
a pig's tail.

I think the weather was better when I was a child.

I put the hailstones in the freezer for posterity, take them out when company comes. My grandpa's hail stones made the newspaper, with measuring tape for scale. A catheterized penis was the last thing I saw of him. And I asked "What's in the center, a fuzzy-wuzzy bear, bubble gum, a pearl, or a rock-hard cock?"

A Pile of Conflicting Emotions about Garbage
(companion 1 to "inside the weather")

Disgust, amusement, joy, curiosity, desire to uncover, pleasure, looking to garbage for clothing and entertainment not food, not yet. Can't eat from it because I get paranoid that food is tainted or rotted or just gross, can wear the dumpstered clothes after washing with brief moments of paranoia because of their unknown origin. The origin of my phobia is clearly connected to the Tylenol murders, I had to check each food item carefully for taint around that time and threw much into the garbage. Bradley, our squatter hero, knows how to comb out the good-to-eat garbage.

An Inventory of
an Elaborate Pile of Garbage
at 2nd Ave. and 2nd St. on June 1, 2000
(companion 2 to "inside the weather")

Blackened tea kettle like one I have at home, couch with living man, eyes closed, his dog and runny dog shit on sidewalk. Cardboard boxes, lamp shade, the filter basket of a drip-o-lator, a wooden serving tray with loose bottom. A mouse's body with eyes open and intact. Styrofoam peanuts. Two balsa wood whiskey bottle boxes, thin wooden fruit basket. Wooden construction walls with POST NO BILLS painted gray. A piece of paper ordering the closing of the Mars Bar garden. A man setting out 4 candles, and 2 sets of wrapped paper plates. A junkie couple, white, late 30s, covered in scabs and tattoos with dog, had constructed a lean-to over the couch and slept that day. I thought about what brought them to this moment and thought "be in the moment," thought "be here now," thought "what's the worse thing that could happen?" Thought "shit happens." And began to think "today is the first day of the rest of . . ." Thought this could be the best day of their lives.

An Early Alphabet

Puritans, Hillbillies, Yankees, Iroquois, Confederates, and Krauts—that's who
made me.

Put in a bird, any bird, even an ugly one, a crow for example
or mention bird anatomy
a wing or feather give it a color
put in a bird, make it fly, let it eat
build a nest
add any bird.

Mention a bird skeleton so delicate and light it flies
mention an egg
mention a bird song
mention a bird's cry
mention a raven's beak boiled
please mention the hair black as the raven's wing I carry in my mouth.

A flock of turkey buzzards, their heads are all red comb, and the bodies. The
ugliest birds I'd ever seen. All my life I'd seen them in the sky, circling. Never on
the ground. I was 38.

I learned to write so I could describe the world
the birdhouse is empty
say something beautiful about it.

To Write It Down

To write their names, to print their names in letters large enough to be seen from a distance to catch someone's eye. To talk about their tattoos or other identification marks, to talk about height and hair and skin color. To find a photograph that someone, a stranger, could recognize them from. To talk about the floor they worked on or the firm they worked for, the last phone call, the last words they spoke to say "Take care of my children" to say "I love you" or to say "the room is full of smoke."

To make a poster about it, to make a poster in case someone should see them or so the world sees them and to call, they might be anywhere, traumatized, unrecognizable, naked, even just to recognize a leg or an arm or a tooth.

To place it in a public place where no one could miss it. On the street at eye level, in a window, on a pole, on the mailbox, on a wall, or in a public park. If there is no place to put it then make a place, others will come and leave flowers and candles. And someone will be by to keep the candles lit, someone will water the flowers and someone will tidy it up.

To describe a personality, to talk about what they liked to do, to talk about whether they liked to cook, or what books they liked to read, to write it down in public the movies they enjoyed, to write down if they liked NYC or if they liked their job or if they were fulfilled. Did they like sports? Did they practice a certain religion? Is there something you could say to make them come alive for us? Some singular trait of individuality or even normalcy.

Be sure to say if they were parents or single or married or divorced. Or write down who is waiting to hear, who is missing them, to write down your cell phone numbers and your home phone. Be sure to write down your name so if someone calls they know who they are speaking to. If the missing has children be sure to include a photograph of them because then strangers will be more likely to respond to your poster.

To you the reader
Be sure to carry a rose to a fire house
to carry a lit candle down the street
to hang a banner
to wear a ribbon
to visit a hospital
to walk by the wall
to read the wall

Then to follow the plume of smoke as close as possible to the source.

III

Diorama

An army of Wal-Mart shoppers in flag motif sweatshirts block the aisle. This is a year of flag displacement.

Dear Diorama,
I'm swimming in a pool of milk becoming butter as we speak.

Dearest Diorama,
I have a dream complete with dirt and sage. It's a Texas of the mind. Life-sized. It's all in my head: a whole landscape made up, crushed and turned to powder. It's a new filmstrip of the West: a bullet of multiple calibers. It's a prickly pear and a sagebrush. A lonesome toothbrush under the pines. I have a Waco of the mind. I'm an army of Jonestown myself. It's in my pants. You know all of it is in my trousers. All of Jonestown is at my lips. I have a little vacation villa set on the edge of the jungle. All of my weapons are secreted there.

We passed the bullets around each taking a bite. The steel between teeth, the chips fell. Empty shell, where you from? No answer. Just a hollow core. A bullet with open mouth, a toothless bullet speaking at the public.

Please be my secret agent.
My A & T & F agent.
My F & B & I informant.
My C & I & A covert operator.
Please be my public servant.
My most private pubic serpent.

I have a box of childs of all shapes and sizes for sale. Some in wheelchairs or still nursing. Some to go or some to stay. Do you want to eat them here?

The children ride in large beetle-shaped carts with faces painted on the front. They ride in a circle around a large toadstool. As for myself, I ride a cart pulled by dogs. It's a good cart with fine, strong dogs straining against the leather. A bark here and a bark there. Up, up, and over the hills and through the midway we go. We are very unusual and good at being who we are but no one will pay to see us.

One day I was out walking and came upon a small container of Janet Reno. She wears a nurse's cape and white starched hat. She wears enough white to pass for Elizabeth Dole. Janet is living in a box. She's in the shape of a TV. All the world is on my TV. World, get off my TV. World, are you listening? World, get off my TV. Well, if you won't get off then please change the channel.

I need a dream to give me some peace.
If I had money, I'd have some peace.
I had 400 dollars once and it gave me some peace.
If I had 450 dollars I'd really be peaceful. Please give!

I was swimming in a pool of milk becoming butter when they approached. They offer 2 childs per milk. I was very busy making the right sort of smooth stroke necessary. I said someone give the childs milk. Someone come get them. Please, please give these childs a home. The Davidians offer 2 meats with toast. Do I want 1 egg or 2? I'm in a shape of Texas.

I'm in a shape of America, come and get me.

THE HUMAN MUSEUM

September 18, 1958, I took the day off to be born.

I be a small girl my bone ringlets not yet fused.
I be a small girl of large proportions
of tremendous feet and little fingers.
I be an Anastasia of wanted and missing posters
of durable DNA.

I have a dress of multiple mirrors
a fork of many flavors
a tongue for attraction after death.
Let me study your folkways and primal hairs. Smile for this gardener gather
leaves and cover the streets.

A bonsai forest grows in Tompkins Square Park.
My animal bone, my animated bones.

I be the smallest child in the human museum. The smallest mouth on earth.
That be me, girl mouth of assorted flowers: bitter and sweet, a cornucopia of
peach stones.

I was eating a child, then the child was eating me. I nearly lost my leg that way.
The long tendons exposed to dirty air. Meanwhile I'm in America wearing a
boutonniere of gigantic proportions.

He enlarged the pond, he did, my brother made the hole bigger and a goldfish
grew the whole circumference round. He stayed in his rooms all those years

only coming out to work and vote. He drove a motored bike, racing trophies all over the room they made of plastic with motorcycled men on top. He built a track in the valley. He made humps of dirt for the bikes to jump. Little children raced with their legs running up and down and jumping off. I'm Queen of the mountain! I'm Queen of the pet rocks and coal mines. Queen of the sassafras and locust. I'm a big Drag King! In my girlhood I was a girl hood. I was a swing set. A bright dish of manic panic properties.

I sell cookies for girls, I sell a girl cookie.

The child brides arrived too soon.
The men tied tin cans to the girls' trains.
They rattle down the hall: small dogs tied to a pole.

Millions of men of 64 flesh-tone crayon colors walked on bones to be here tonight. The girls shine oyster shells in the moonlight. Buttons of their teeth given to the men for vests and trousers. They said girls bow down and serve. Even the youngest open wide. I went searching for the killers. I wore only one glove. I was a lawyer, now I have a talk show. We talk about the law and there are a lot of laws to talk about. But first we're going to visit the early hairdos of the O.J. Simpson trial.

She be a small girl-child with box-cutter scars on her face, cut by other girls. She's a small girl-child of the goodest kind.

Please let me into your home.
I sell cleaners for the house and car.
I sell pot holders, seeds, dope, smoke, and blue-green algae.
I'm a spokesmodel for God. Let me in.
I'm God's spokesmodel,
Please forgive me.

The Blue Eye: A Paper Film

3 mins. Color. Instructions: Open with shots of water, then the faces of all animals from our houses and their eyes, singular and in pairs. Go to pens and pastures recording eyes of every sort: the domestic and the indigenous: dogs, cats, hamsters, horses, cows, pigs, goats, and birds.

Narrative to be read aloud: There existed in the world a single blue eye. It belonged to a face. The face was beautiful and still living even though the eye had been lanced out. The eye lay in a jar. The jar sat on a table in a lab. White coats came and took it places. It watched. It went many places and saw many things. It saw you and it saw me.

Film all sorts of texts: bibles, napkins, matchbooks, notebooks, receipts, scraps. It had a little DNA. Inside the DNA was a story. To get the story, the eye was pulverized. The story went back to black. The story was traced by the white coats. They made a film. The film said water. It said salt and it said dirt. It even said weather and it said stars. *End with a black frame.*

Personal to Reader/Viewer: I'll film your eye in head, of course. And any eye-like image. Belly button, triangle, peephole, or viewmaster. I'd like a good eye looking out at the Ohio River. I'd build a kaleidoscope made of butterfly wings and small gravel fossils. Later record the eyes open out to horizons of corn (6 feet high with tasseled sexed tops). Their arm blades, each kernel an eye, an eye bank. Eaten.

A Short Story That Takes Place on the Moon

That night I began this story again. It happened like this: a wallet belonging to the previous tenant arrived in the mail. It was fat and full of identification and contained many pictures. The pictures were of places close up and far away.

Each year the moon moves farther away. In some places the dust is 60 feet straight down. A man put his foot and his flag on it, spoke words and then rocketed home in a silver bottle. On his way he saw other planets, including Venus. He knew it would not be colonized soon. Later a silver suit hung on the door and he was home.

A fat wallet came to the apartment bulging with information and empty of cash. The owner had left them many things. His bed even. It had a drawer under it. A mouse had made a nest there. The walls of the apartments were beige. The kitchen had an old-fashioned smallish metal-topped table. His mail continued to arrive, later flowers came.

The moon is just a dusty orb ringing around the earth locked into an eternal orbit. The earth is ringing its way around the sun. All around the moon is quiet. Silent ornaments surround the sun.

It's quiet here, only soft traffic noise exists. Only astronauts.

The captain's chair is nice for driving through space, but I prefer a real couch or some sort of big, solid American furniture, heavy, life-like—something that suggests commitment because of the weight and trouble of moving such a big object. A piece under plastic or with proper care could outlast even the beings who first conceived of it as an idea.

I'm lifting heavy furniture on the moon.

Your 60s cult was uncovered. All they did was collect weapons and make paper-work. Although making paperwork is an honorable profession and it's difficult to come up with good questions like: What's your name? Address? Social Security Number?

Oh yes, my weapon collecting.
I lost my weapons.
Now I roam with only two legs and no armies.

There is distant paperwork due on other planets.

My cult consists of quilt makers. It's the busiest work I could devise.
Our cult of quilts is an Amish extravaganza.

Yo followers
Yo quilters
Yo pushcarts
Yo peddlers
Yo panhandlers
Yo homeboys
Yo in the dress
Yo on the blades
Yo in the squats
Yo in subways
Please join my astral revolution.

LECTURE #1

My hand bones were life-sized, my feet bones were life-sized, my leg bones, my thigh bones, my hip bones & backbones, my neck bones, and skull bones, life-sized, my arms, my finger bones. All of me was life-sized. I was astonished by my life-like appearance.

Would you care for a thyroid?

Today we are going to make soap. We'll need fat and lye. I hope you've brought your own animal. Now for my fourth human feature, I'd like to present my cleft palate. In addition to showing you my mildly recessive dormant genes.

Hello Numerous Love Objects.
Numerous Love Objects please make yourselves known.
Refuse to be incognito!

Ladies & Gentlepersons, may I have your attention. For my 5th and final human feature tonight, I'd like to present a rare case of gargoylism. If you'll turn your attention to the flying buttress overhead you'll see . . .

Today we will compare and contrast three things: a wheel & a bird & a tree. I think that a wheel is like a bird because it constantly returns home. I believe that a bird is like a tree because if a bird sits still for a long time a tree will grow from its back. If that tree stands still and tall for a very long time, it will turn into a wheel. I think a tree is a wheel. I think a wheel is a bird; however, a wheel is not like a bird. A wheel is not like a tree. In fact, the wheel does not even like the bird, and the wheel does not like the tree. The wheel prefers primates and reptiles to the family of birds or the family of trees. The tree feels the same only is more passionate about its dislikes. The tree accepts the bird and the wheel. It needs the birds. But the birds hate the leaves and the birds love the sky. The birds, the birds, they love a wheel of cheese.

DR. WASSERMAN

I lay out the sheet: Square, square, triangle, cave, cave-in-rock, mound, dirt, shell, sand, rock, crab, leaf, mite, moth, rat, and roach. Hoe, hoe, and hoe. I straighten & quilt & quilt, row & row, knife & knife, knit & knit, pearl & pearl all along Avenue B. This is sex work.

A viewing box was ready. So the viewing began.
Look in the hole. (Small pictures of Robert Frank fly by. I wrote to him on his pictures. On all his pictures, I wrote "Stop, go ahead.")

I was in conversation with Hellen Keller. We placed our hands on our mouths and read the following letter together: "T."

A small dominatrix wrote a book about sexual working. She had a concubine, a dog, and a boy-child on a tether. He makes wood for her. He can make wood on the mattress. He's in his room making the walls. He makes a dining room set, a wardrobe, an end table. He's going to make her a forest. A grove of birches. Birch barks & scrolls. His wood leafs off into fingers.

A branch leafs toward water.
Make me a fire. Make me a breaker 1-9.

I was a citizen's band and banned by the citizens for my sex working. It took all my time. I rolled quarters in a sock and wore them in my hat. I made the wood and I was happy to see me. I made the wood from lint. A balsam log soft and lodged in my beret. I sex work at night with myself. Do I a queen or worker be? My leather work was contained in a trailer. I was working toward my manhood. I wanted a new menshood. One not pierced, cut, and penetrated but a whole cloth.

A Stick

I needed a stick for guidance. Navigation is important for getting a girl over the
seas. I had carried my branch since I was a child, needing it in these Americas.
In my hand, a many-branched olive tree, of thee I sang, of Christ who kneeled
beneath it.

I had a war. Inside, all my channels were turned to one station.
I afeared that war, it made a wall of wreaths, ribbons, quilts.
It took organs and bloods.
It took trees.
It left cancers and bones.
Soldiers came back to America, back to me as small flags.

I was scared.
In my palm, tiny boats floated.
Across my fingertips tiny boats sailed.

Boy Eye

My film began this way: A park on the East River, 4th of July.
Three fat ladies on the ground doing leg lifts and laughing. I bought a Pepsi.

I didn't know where to begin with recording the world so I started with skin.
Then entire bodies, later rocks and flowers. Then onto gardens. There was
land, water, and aluminum cans, barges, sea planes, and plastics yet to be
recorded. I said I'd record every kind of animal 2 by 4. I went into this hoping
to save something, like memory or coupons. I was trying to make sight impor-
tant. I was making it important to see. I was making it important to describe. I
was becoming a seeing eye artist.

In the park were men in go-carts, wheelchairs, and on foot. When news arrived
of the third eye, I was elated. My foray into experimental organs had begun. I
would be like the mechanical heart man, only I would have a fine eye. A boy's
eye implanted on my forehead.

The eye arrived in a thermos of ice. My cold eye on rocks. Laid on ice like an
oyster. I didn't kill the boy myself, he died natural and I didn't harvest it. I only
ordered it through the mail from the back of a driver's license.

With the eye I saw people walking toward fireworks. I could see them all fully
clothed but they could see me naked. It was very exciting to be totally naked in
a crowd while wearing three eyes.

Soon the third eye atrophied. It had a reverse effect. Instead of recording the
world the eye looked inward.

What did it see?

It saw highways. It saw rock cairns, piles of stones from the sea. It saw the last formations of the mound builders. It saw me mound building. I was very busy. I was building a shrine. I was making mounds for viewing. It was important for seeing.

What was your work? What was important to do?

It was important to walk across the Brooklyn Bridge at midnight, to thrift shop all fifty states and to ride a bike. It was important to hang out and be there. Being there was the best part. I was part of a history. I was a woman, I think. I was with other writers and we were working toward a collective vision, a melee of language and symbols. We were bookmaking. Our hands were speaking and collecting. The hands were breaking sound. It was important to write poems. It was important to hear music and eat. Sex was, sleeping was. Reading books, that was important, but most of all it was important to see you.

Forecasting

I'm writing to tell you that my xeroxing skills have improved greatly. I can color copy almost anything but I mainly duplicate coins. I won't get rich all at once, instead I'll slowly accumulate wealth while avoiding detection. I'll acclimate to a higher economic standard, and you know that if my great ship docks, you're flush with me. By the way, do you have a penny wrapper? My new copying skills are sure to bring fame and multiple jobs. Of that I'm sure, besides I have already invested in tree futures. Of the trees' future, I do not know. I mean I'm not sure if there's a future for the trees.

THE THREE MEN

These three men are saluting America. They love what they do and they have a good time. They could enjoy themselves anywhere, and anyplace especially if they were being told what to do. If they were in a war they would enjoy themselves more than winning at bowling and more than winning at gambling. It would be better to be told to wear camouflage than to drink free whiskeys all night in a tavern. In the tavern there are bags of chips behind the bar, but they would rather be fighting than eating bags of chips. In the bar there is a radio on the shelf. They prefer to arm wrestle rather than listen to radio. They would like to be told what the mission is and be given all they need to carry it out. They need direction from superiors. It's good to be bossed. They would much rather be bossed than enjoy themselves. Well, actually they'd rather enjoy being killed.

WEATHER REPORT

PROLOGUE:
The Rain Fell Hard on the Jacqueline Kennedy Onassis Auction

I have car leathers to be nourished and shielded from the sun. I have mildewed interiors, carpets to be fluffed and dried. Where's my special knob? I'm driving cross country and I'm in climate control.

I'm walking around with divining rods in both fists finding underground weathers. These sewers are confusing. Your divining fists are annoying.
Shh! (listen) A barometer falls in Queens.

A patch of water fell.
A patch of water fell on my head.

I want to speak of various weathers. I've been surfing these subways and buses, I've been on foot in search of webs of . . . moist (data). I'm going to be doing some casting here, stand back! Look out for the hook. Ooops!

A small creek ran just under the surface of the rock, showing up now and again to present its body to us. We were in then, making buoyant markers in a body, water leaching out from rock, sand tablets, limestone. A Hoosier rock, a quarry, a building, these waters. This water presenting its face.

The Day of My Most Favorite Weather

I was en route to my jobs when I experienced a panorama of weatherly-responsive gifted clouds, flying like skywriters, hurling good wishes. After each job, during the few minutes between work, excellent weather followed my train under the river, good weather alongside, clear in the tunnels. "It's dry in this cave today," said the other passengers while closing their umbrellas.

Good weather in the Texas Fried Chicken restaurant across from the jobs and the works. Good, clear mirror in the bathroom, a light mist rose from the mashed potatoes, a little precipitation of Coca-Cola overhead.

Best Weather That I Remember

Ahh!

BLACK BOXES

Many things fall from the sky.
A jet has a big body.
It's long and heavy and made of metal and plastic.

Robert went into a tunnel of homelessness.
They were having lots of sex—all kinds.
It was dark but he could see in glimpses.
A woman emerged, beautiful. Herself stank.

I ate the box.
It went down, stayed inside, and made notes on all our speeches.
I have the entire transcript of our social intercourse.

Extracting the boxes from the ocean floor is difficult.
The conversations of fishes and marine life are indecipherable
as they do not have an alphabet.

Capitalist Projections

O Projector! O film still!

My capitalist projector needs repair. The frames keep speeding up.
Everything whirs by in a blur. I need a rock or a stick to slow it down.

So go on & break the wheel, break the spokes, the lens, put out the light.

The bowling strikes arrive quicker than light. Could you roll back to the 60s
and fetch the milk? I don't want the hormone kind, but if I must. When you
were in the 60s couldn't you have saved me a place? It was cheap. You could have
done something for me. This money asks for something. This money asks that
something be done. So do something.

Look, I died young. I was following the money. It asked a lot of me and I gave.
I threw it a bone. The price of money rose, it can't be quenched. It's got a long
drink . . . a thirst.

I'd like to see that bone. I should have asked to keep it. It could have stayed in
a box on virgin vinyl. It wouldn't have taken a lot of room. It's no femur. Just a
vertebra. I could have buried it with me. We'd rest on my grandma's grave. I'd be
in a little box, my bone an amulet of DNA on top. However my plan is to be
ashes, my bones are to be bird stones.

Millennium Day

I prefer to remain, while others catch a ride on a bright and rare comet, and it makes me sad to be wearing such ugly brown earth shoes.

THE KILLING THIEF IN THE NIGHT

In this paragraph appears the quietest killer
Silence, who is the killing thief in the night.
"A killing thief who takes," said the sad priest.

"Silence, you who visits unsuspecting sleepers in their sheets,
you are dangerous. I heard crickets and locusts announce your name."

Silence was on the tip of insect tongues
in the prairie, so I listened there.

DUMPSTER

My mission is to gather intelligence, so I went to the dumpster. There! Exactly what I was looking for. I washed it first before putting it on, it looks good on me. I'm not afraid of polyester. I'm not afraid of mixing prints. This is not a mere shirt. This is evidence.

My task is to investigate the special prosecutor. He seeks and seeks and yet his case is just a ghost. I can't get through to him. He's tied up on the phone line, he's found the 1-900 Psychic Family. The Magic 8-Ball says try again later. The name Monica floats in inky water. Inside the 8-ball it's dark and warm. He is not dissuaded from finding the truth. He is not dissuaded by lack of evidence. His only qualification is his suspicion.

I spread tea leaves over the landfill so I can read Fresh Kills. These mounds tell all. I can foretell the future potential of the garbage barge. Is there one in your future? I see it clearly on the mound of Venus. You're going on a cruise of sensuous decay.

My favorite dumpster memory: hundreds of bowling balls in assorted colors— too heavy to carry through Manhattan. They would have to be thrown.

I remember the green green of dumpsters, the fields of them freshly born. Dumpsters as pure as milk. "Every day is like Christmas," said the garbage man as he collected my weekly gift. I remember sitting among mating rats in Tompkins Square piss-soaked park. I told them telepathically I'm very happy about the president fucking and being blown and so is America. I thought, this is great. This synchronicity of fucking between rats and our highest servant. "Rats," I asked, "Can I join your psychic family?"

Memory Jar

It's all solid blocks of pain. Why go there and do that? Memory is meant to be forgotten, rewritten in order to bear. It's not even terrible, only the passage of time hurts. I can't bear all the years falling off the calendar, each moving faster and swifter, the body slower or perhaps the body losing out to time.

I'm collecting pot shards and glass for a memory walk, a sidewalk encrusted with literal memory, sharp and dangerous until worn down. Objects created strictly for the purpose of remembering. A memory jug covered in gold paint and beads. A rug woven of my great-uncle's police clothes. A crazy quilt top with fancy stitches. A statue of Mary, boxed, ornate, her head chipped off. Herself beheaded during moving. My head that broke off in a car wreck got mended, and you can't tell it was ever broke by looking.

The cast of Buster's arm, broken falling off a ladder in the hayloft. Near death mementos, my neck brace and accident clothes. I have the shoe that survived, the black vintage western shirt with snaps cut off at the hospital. The scissor cuts are jagged, it was good cotton.

My grandfather's meat case is full of bird nests.
Is this my reliquary box?
What bone have I placed there?
My foot box is filled with horse hooves.
My head box is filled with horse hair.
I won't describe the intricate urns and vessels I have built to carry the soft organs into eternity.

Proof exists in the smallest and most mundane of gestures. Shadows, the smell of flowers, electrical shorts, mirror reflections. It's the most rational and common acts that yield evidence of the spirit.

Time Near the End of Time

Elaborate roadside shrines erupt like morels in spring. A Harley flag tied to an oil stick marks the spot. I found a metal cross under the underpass and marked in steel was Robert, 1971-1998. Here is a marker for a boy who didn't make it to the end of the millennium. He could have ushered in the new century when all the computers turned over and blew up.

The metal numbers of a pre-digital clock flipped over at the time of his conception.

He broke his neck or else it was a case of rapture, because in a case of rapture the driver will be missing and the car will weave and crash into sinners because God doesn't care about sinners. A hundred years ago the boy could have died in a buggy crash perhaps. The repair for crushed vertebrae was so unreliable, not like now, when the repair of bodies is to the point of reattaching and replacing parts. Before you were like a horse, a broken leg is grounds for shooting.

A flag at half-mast.

In 1934, his great-great-uncle got drunk and drove a car with sideboards, and maybe with chrome streamlined hubcaps, into a train. Perhaps a black train and a black car. He killed all his friends, too, in one rapture-like action. Perhaps God needed some coal miners and drunks in heaven in the same way he needed a pickax murderer. Who needs us in heaven besides ourselves?

God is counting the hairs on his head.
Can a forest be sad? If it could be, it would be.

The boy exploded the truck in Indianapolis, left the road, hit the tracks too hard, he was always afraid that he'd miss somebody partying. Maybe the twin boys pulling a bottle from the crack of the couch. Partying is as important a reason to be here as anything else.

Being the life of a party, he knew his calling: Why was I put on earth? To party and to drive a big truck. How come some people don't make it past their partying years? Just dumb luck.

He hated to fly, he preferred the ground and traveled by land and not the sea either. He hated to travel by sea because the ocean is just the sky in reverse, vast and uncharted. The ocean is just the sky manifested in liquid particles. The sea is worse than sky—where fish eat you, or you'll be wrinkled like your fingertips or vulva or resting cock, all over. I do not believe my flotation seat cushion will save me.

As time nears the end of time, what urns should he carry with him? An urn filled with electronics for the passage; a cell phone for the tunnel, solar-powered for heaven. For hell, bring extra batteries.

As for myself, I would like to carry the same things a pelican does in her pouch. What I really want is a built-in flap of tissue instead of a purse. A flesh purse, yes, a flesh purse. A carryall.

I have the feeling that hell is damp, never wet, only thickly humid like Indiana in the summer. Not a dry heat like Las Vegas, where you die just trying to walk into a casino from the mega-parking lot. I like the deserts of Las Vegas, if hell were that I'd be happy. If hell had green lichen the shade of a faded dollar bill, I'd be happy. Because as they say hell is what you make it.

He's sorry he was late, he got caught in a traffic jam of souls en route to places out yonder. This is what happens when everyone tries to leave all at once.

A Sightseeing Tour

On the first night at the band shell, a gospel band celebrated the end of time.
They were praying and singing that a huge asteroid would hit the earth.
They sounded very wistful, If only a big comet would come and vindicate us.

She always wanted to turn the barn into their real house when they retired.
Every time she goes out there that's what she says and recites all the names of
the rooms: living room, dining room, bedroom, and the great room. Or maybe
she'll just keep it all open, just one big room with haylofts and hoisting beams
and ladders just the way they are. She lives just to go out to the back and say
the names. If you can say the words the rooms become real. She really believes
that if you can name it you can own it. She believes that her trouble stems from
never having asked the universe to grant her wishes.

There was a 60-ft tall Santa that marked the turn off to Holiday World. Over the
summer he was painted into King Kong and rented out to grand openings. If you
see either Santa or King Kong, please remember they are one and the same.

As are:
Buffaloville
Newtonville
Yankeeville
Patronville
Owensville &
The McDonald's in Boonville *"Where Lincoln learned the law."*

For their honeymoon they went to the Amish theme park. The Amish had stripped off a hill, flattened it, and laid down a fake town of crafts shops and a huge restaurant called *The Gasthof*. They slowed down to watch some Amish kids fishing in a runoff creek. The boys were wearing polyester work pants, homemade with buttons like on a sailor's bell bottoms. The girls wore plain dresses with white gauze bonnets covering their heads.

If you need a barn raised, call them. The Amish can put up a barn in a day. If you want hell raised, call my Aunt Wilma.

A retarded man lived across the field from a normal man who killed his parents 20 years ago, the retarded man said that the normal man seemed okay to him, later everyone found out different. When they entered the house they found locks on the inside of the parents' bedroom. Still, he got them and then his grandmother in the tub with scissors.

Youngblood Funeral Home is where everyone in town goes for the free calendars and matches. That's who will embalm us, the son, Lonnie Youngblood Jr. We know where we'll go and who will do us, but we don't know who put the "balm" in embalm.

My old neighbors used to bathe in a galvanized tub in the kitchen and melt saccharine in a teaspoon for their coffee. They watched *Dark Shadows* a scary TV show in the garage. His wife chased my aunt out of the orchard, a small strip of worthless land they feuded over. They won, yet never cultivated the fruit.

IV

A Horseless Carriage

Since then—'tis Centuries—and yet
Feels shorter than the Day
I first surmised the Horse Heads
Were toward eternity
—FROM 712, EMILY DICKINSON

We traded some hay and got a pony
But we were horseless

We got a good deal on a horse
We were full with the horse

The horse was an asshole
We sold the horse

We bought a car
But we were horseless

I remember all the grave mowers. I used to follow Elise and his mules to the cemetery. They were majestic. Mules are pretty, people forget that. When he died I bought the old harnesses at auction. People took horse collars and put mirrors where the heads used to go. That was a fad. Everyone had harness and leather lying around that they needed to put some use to. Old oil lamps, railroad lanterns, these things look good with a plant sticking out of them. I once buried a treasure in Elise's meadow. I had been reading about pirates. I was obsessed with finding buried treasure, since there was scant chance of finding buried treasure on a landlocked farm. I decided to make a mystery imagining someone finding it and wondering about whoever buried it. I took a cardboard box, put clues in it, a penny minted that year, a picture of me and my brother, a metal picture frame with curlicues that I now realize was Victorian. Once the field grew over, I could never find it again.

Tom, down the road, sold his horse buggies when I was a kid and I remember everyone talking about the auction. The buggies. Black carriages, stiff. Horseless now. Motorless. The end of buggies except for the Amish's yellow, black, and white tops.

There was Old Man Hinkle who drove his horseless carriage so slowly that I'd pass him on my bike. He was headed down the road to where Herb and Buster held court on the front lawn in shell-backed lawn chairs. Mary and Tootsie were in the house, a glass butter churn on the table. I had summer habits that kept me on the road, popping tar bubbles with a stick. Breaking ponies. Fishing. Exploring. The world could be as long as a mile or two. It was all the way around, follow the road until you were back to where you began.

My grandparents were horseless, by the time I knew them. I have a dim photo of my grandpa driving a carriage. My grandma didn't drive anything as far as I could tell, but she did like to call a bicycle "a wheel." As in "Where you going on that wheel?" Or "Put that wheel down and get over here." Or "Hey, you on the wheel, come back here." It was a uniquely horseless form of transportation.

Two farmers in abutting pastures died this fall. Neither of them owned horses. Cody, in his 60s, died of skin cancer that metastasized into brain cancer. Harold, 83, who inherited the job from Elise, and meticulously mowed the cemetery with a tractor, died of stomach cancer this winter one month shy of the end of the century. Last summer, he wanted his usual garden put out. They put out a smaller one, knowing he'd never be able to see it. Now, as it snows, I walk toward his grave. I imagine all of us, long-horseless, walking.

THE CAT SITUATION

A 2nd set of newborn cats, born and abandoned. She had them in a cat carrier right outside the kitchen door where the flies are. Mom said that the flies would lay eggs on them, and they will die from the parasites. Or starve, since none of the cats will claim the kittens and all of the female cats that we can observe are pregnant. Last week the black-and-white cat had four kittens in the abandoned Toyota. She didn't clean them off, refused to watch them, and by morning the hind legs had been eaten off of one. Of course they were all dead. A sad relief, that was four fewer kittens to tame and get rid of, and now the black-and-white cat could be neutered.

In my parents' time, they just shot them or put them in a sack and tossed them in a creek. We used to drive by Little Pigeon Creek and see a floating bag. Dad said they were puppies or kittens. Folks did not invest in animals the way they do now. During the past ten years, my parents began to take the animals to the vet; animals who would have been cured by bullet. My father died Christmas night after a long illness and my mom had let the cat situation get out of hand. They were originally three females that he rescued from a dumpster over a decade ago. They gave him companionship in the barn, which was their domain, no dogs were allowed entry. In the winter, they sat with him in front of the wood burner. There are 17 cats as of this writing, mostly half-feral (defined as can be touched while eating or just brushed with a hand without running off or snarling), and 5 of them are female kittens too wild to touch.

The kittens survived. Mom had gone out in the night and placed cardboard over the carrier to keep midnight rain out. This morning she found a new kitten, with afterbirth the size of the kitten itself, attached to the end of the umbilical cord. I snipped it off. Later in the week, in the time it took me to walk to the barn and back, one kitten was shook to death by an unknown assailant, the others had also been severely attacked. We waited for their mother to return, when she didn't we took them inside to nurse. They had internal injuries, and flies had laid larvae in the wounds. We spent the night nursing them with a special bottle and powdered formula, but none of them could swallow nor understand what was requested of them. The next morning we called a neighbor man to kill them as swiftly as possible. He had offered to kill unwanted cats and dogs for the old farm ladies since in the last year that entire generation of husbands had passed away. I couldn't see making the kittens suffer another day, but could also feel how much they wanted to live, and I cried for their suffering.

Later I pretended with the curtain closed on his room that he was asleep. Also felt him so much present that I didn't miss him, and because I knew my own body and emotions. I was a part of him, a splinter of DNA. Day ended with me, mom, and sister sitting outside kitchen door, butterfly landed twice on my finger.

BURIALS

I am to be buried on top of my grandmother's grave in the Bloomfield cemetery looking out over a pasture. In the pasture is a large tree that cows shade themselves under in the summer. I thought that tree would outlast me, but it was felled by lightning.

One time, I went driving with a friend who said that he wanted to be buried because he wanted a stone marker as proof that he had lived on the planet. Myself, I don't care, it hasn't been important to leave a mark, rather it's the absence of marks I'm concerned with.

I buried a goldfish in a matchbox under the split maple tree. The ground was difficult to break through, full of roots and hard-packed dirt. I dug with a spoon and butter knife, several inches down, saving the dirt for cover; knowing that the hole would take more than what I removed, how it would sink down, and I'd end up laying a stone on top.

I've made holes of different sorts. Some for planting bulbs, or trees, even for fence posts with a special digger, using my weight on the blade, my feet working the top, slicing off the inches of soil, snapping through roots, making each hole squared, clean, and sized to fit the object to be planted or buried. My father was strong and could dig a fine hole. I admired his biceps and wanted them myself.

I wrapped the stray in Karla's yard in two garbage bags and dug the hole round after the animal's curled-up posture. Placed two bricks on top and filled with dirt, and patched with the squares of grass I had cut and lifted anticipating the need for a smooth finish. Still I didn't quite get it right—the hole sunk in a few days even with the bricks, but no matter, the dogs didn't get to it and that was the main aim.

The winter of my recovery, the dogs dragged around a pair of front legs from the neighbor's dead mule. The mule had died of loneliness in the fall. The neighbor man let it lie in its stall till he could get around to it, but winter came; a hard cold that hadn't been felt in years. The ground froze too solid for burial. The legs were unrecognizable. At first, they looked like stripped green branches, then came the stench, then the weight of damp bones, stripped of skin and meat. The hooves were left on like hard shoes. It took several minutes to see them as legs.

We marked Rusty's grave with an old concrete slab from across the road. It was white and embedded with pennies. We would spend hours filing away at it hoping to get one freed to take to the store so we could buy a penny candy. That slab is covered over with roots now. It sank down under the sassafras and was bound up in the roots of an old wild rosebush.

My aunt was exhumed by my mother and father. After my grandfather died my grandmother wanted her daughter who died as an infant brought over to the family plot. She was buried in Bullock Town during the depression, a flower bush marked her grave. She couldn't drink milk, she just starved, really. She'd been buried in a small box with brass handles they placed in a crate my grandpa had around his old store, and that's all they found. Two brass handles and rich dark dirt.

V

A Book

If you were in prison what would you do?

I was in prison writing my memoirs. I wrote with a shiv, a cloth wound around a blade, fastened from a plastic utensil. Writing this way I turned the text into wood. I carved license plates out of soap. This worked very well until it rained. I think you're washing with one now. Does it say 82 Frank 359? I carved out my own special messages, "Hello" and "Stop the Gentrification Plague" (SGP).

A wall of license plates in Midway, Indiana, has rusted up and gone back to ore. My soap plates have gone back to animals, they've gone back to fat. I went back. I went back to dirt. I went back to black holes.

CALENDAR

On this date I saw a star, a daytime star rocket to earth. I saw with my two hands that a glorious light had landed. It made a crop circle in the shape of my dream. It was a dream of triangles and hexagrams in the wheat. Two boys had made it, they mowed down the grass with a log into an interlocking circle, perfect without a stem out of place.

Roll down the wheat, roll down the corn. It was perfect circles.

An Estate Sale

PREAMBLE:

Two serious clairvoyants were taking tea.
The most serious took my hand. The less serious took my astral hand.
Together they tried to guess my weight and height.

My estate is mainly composed of intricate weaving. Nuns, as you know, wove during their sleep. They wove delicate flowers into wreaths and macramé hanging baskets. The Brontës wore bracelets and chains made of hair. They drove themselves nearly bald.

To collect such hairs would be time-consuming, but there was no collecting, just them falling into a receiver: a round powder box with a hole in the center. A wonderful device for placing the hair away. All of mine were donated to a maker of merkins. A pubic patch of exquisite natural fibers. A miniature trellis of dread knots. I was fleeced, really! I should be receiving, instead I'm giving.

Nothing is as precise as a hair. You think it's a novel with plots and characters, but it's only hair weavings. However, it's not fat dreads oiled up into a wick and lit aflame.

SEEDHEAD

Are we on time for the mixed breed competition? I entered as a hybrid. My human gene was spliced into a watermelon. The melon cries when cut. My sheep are organ trees.

Mr. Sheep I'd like to get to know you. Hey, I mean we're gonna be close, like really really close. Hey you who bear my spare liver, put down that whiskey! And don't eat any red meat. I'm counting on those heart valves. (Sniff) I've really become a swine.

(sniff) Hummmm. I smell truffles.

I'm an entirely new animal now. I am a descendant of Anglo-Saxon-swine-sheep-bovine-extraction.

I am driving the car as a new species, of a new mammal. Do I need a license for this?

I'm out harvesting organs. My wagon is full of kidneys. Loaded to the brim with hearts all pumping. It's a briny wagon of swimming muscle. Look at the muscles flexing, moving before the thought of moving. The muscle moving beneath us like super underwear.

Will you wager a guess? Will you wager a guess on how many kidney stones are in my jar?

Hayroll

This hayroll rolled home. See, here, this vomited a calf. Hail hayball in the shape of Mary. A virgin hayball of timothy grass. I've been watching these balls glow at dusk. That one is a thief, this one is a Christ, and the other is a snowball.

I rolled you away and rose myself. It's dark in this home of dirt, this caving, vena cava, bloody home. I watch dueling hayballs through the stereoscope. They double and move during the night, even at day they have no sense of absurdity.

This has been my life weaving a home out of poor materials. How would I keep out the elements, the wolf and the police? This straw house is breaking my back. My heap of house of grasses, I love you because you're what I've found in this life. Such poor building blocks, would they make a safe home? Could I be a strong house? I look in the mirror and ask, Are you really? Are you really a future farmer of America?

The straw floss between my lips . . . cud . . . not . . . chew . . .
it.   Huge ball of hay in my belly.

My favorite farmer rolls hayballs up my beautiful ass.

Hayroll hell no! Cinnamon roll!

I photographed the ball yesterday. I had seen a hawk sitting on top as mother and I drove by. This singular hayball was rolled there by goddess farmers or coughed up by the Future Farmers of America.

My lens is round and so is the ball. Let's look at it in perspective: a silo over the hill, a creek and line of trees framing the mown field. A single cow eats this single ball. A single mother will eat this single burger.

Hayhenge

This megalithic rotunda of balls
fills the courthouses fills the Wal-Marts fills the shelters fills
the outhouses fills the trailer parks.

I can barely see over these balls . . . I don't think any human could have rolled
them here, how could there be such balls all alone, they couldn't be man-made.
They must be woman-made. America is filled with balls. I noticed while stand-
ing on this great earth. Thinking about the suspension of these planets and
stars. What rocky fiery balls they are burning through this dark.

This be the greatest poem ever written about asteroids and hayballs.

Third Farming Poem

The bony cow of youth walked by.
Queen candidates trod through the mud and straw.
On top of the pump house lay blue and brown eggs, in layers of hen shit.
Beautiful spheres.

Shock of corn, shelled peas, shucked beans, plucked turnips

The shape of these farmers. It's amazing!
They strode like milk cartons down the midway, boxy and white, a curdled flow
of cream.
How could I dress them?
Paint them?
Film them?
Can a camera see them?

Can you see my dairy maids? Can you see my groomsmen? Wait here while I
remove my corn belt.

At the heart of America is a wrathbone, a wishbone split into this blue,
broken boner.

A Summer Newsreel

I

After the flood, the books before the Bible drift by. You can still find them float-ing. You still find sinners floating and arks (boats) burning (that is why animals learned to swim, they had a lot of practice).

It occurs to me that I've dressed too blue: wallet, shirt, pants, checkbook, shoes. All accessories in blue. I'm embarrassed. Bought pastels today and a new pen—blue because I need to master this world of blue.

Looking at real estate ads in Canyeville, Kentucky, where my ancestors lived. Only pictures of ranch brick houses, nothing of coal mines. Not a starter mine or mine that needs TLC.

I must have went far into the dirt not finding China but shed, pit, bucket, oil, and ash heap. I've never been to Caneyville. It must be blue coal mines.

In this poem lots o' reading is occurring. I read while writing this. I read this in blue shirt with light blue and green and yellow swirly patterns with faded painter pants.

II

This is the almost last summer of this century in a town where our streets, laid out in 1876, were left off the late 20th-century surveyor's map.

Why am I writing about maps when Indiana is bursting beneath my feet stained purple with mulberries?

The crickets hum louder than the TV. Father's oxygen sounds like running water, like a stream. Stream o' life for him. He sits or lies down.

Brenda sorts through boxes in the attic.
Mom plants a flower.
The dogs sleep under the car.
The cats breed and kill.

As for the Coultases you can take them or leave 'em. They either get skinnier or chunky at midlife. As for them, well, they'd rather be left out of any poem.

So many would like to be Brenda Coultas, chewing and spitting tobacco like a grasshopper.

So many people would like to be her, making taffy all summer and living near Holiday World where every day is a holiday. So many would like to be her living near. So many would love to be her at the drive-in with 6 screens and her own car. So many of you would like to be me with your own car.

At the Rockport cemetery stands a headstone shaped like a horse. An entire horse, not a horse bust or just horse penis but the full body of my friend who fucked a girl there in the cemetery. A living girl on a blanket that she carried in her car, and now I pause to think of the horse.

What will the Coultas family do today? Mom will fry bacon. Dad will work a crossword puzzle. The entire family will mow again and plant one mum.

For so many, I'm going to do today what they wish they could do for themselves.
Breathing
walking
driving
eating
turning on lights & growing turnips.

Is there something that you would like me to do today?
Is there something Brenda Coultas can do for you? She would like to help you. She is reading and writing and stopping to serve you. Everyone is robed in burlap. Brenda Coultas covered you in quilts while you were singing.

III

All hail to July
All hail to UMW, All hail to my bituminous friends.
Hail to the McCoy house now torn down, with whitewashed trees
leaving the branches with nothing to embrace.

Silk down of milkweed carries seeds of summer.
Abe's mother and I drank a poisoned milk.

So happy are the berries to see us. The carrots and potatoes are
thrilled.

Nude blackberry pickers learned their lesson. They are invisible amongst the
bushes stained purple, amongst the garden tools: rakes, hoes, pitchforks, and
scythes are nude-friendly equipment.

So nude the farmers on John Deere combines, reapers of corn, now reapers of
men. Foolish nudes among the yarrow, so beautiful but, alas, so sadly foolish.

IV

Thunder & stars
wheat fields all brown, abundant
at dark, no colors
just the sky is colored.
The dogs invisible and colored like night.

A summer flood hits river bottoms. Old trailers on pilings drift away.

A car floats down the white river, no one driving underwater or swimming alongside. Is the car breaking all the rules by swimming alone?

My niece gets her first period. Could that be in a poem or piece of writing? That is an easy thing to write. Can she visit Holiday World on the first day? Is having a period like a holiday every day? Can virgins go to Holiday World happy? My mind is unpenetrated yet halved, just the same and bleeding and happy like today is a holiday.

Santa Claus lives in Holiday World, where boys and girls sit on
his lap wishing for toys and less anxiety about being good. In a
glass case is a magic village where it's Christmas to this very
day, and a wax museum of our favorite founding fathers. Their skin
and thoughts are pure as waxed floors, their eyes pure glass
reflection.

If the forest is no longer virgin, then what is it? If I am no
longer virgin, then what am I? So broken inside. I am so broken
inside, a Shaker's spiritual hymen.

My heart is not dark, not dark. Only tired.

Could all these things be? Where could all these things be? The answer: inside a salt shaker, especially the turtle-shaped one that shakes salt from this head: the top of this head dispenses salt. Were the Shakers right and should I make this poem as perfect as a Shaker broom (chair?) or bread? Should this poem be perfect for God—do you belong to God?

Reader, are you perfect enough? Are you perfect enough for God?

There is no more Shaker pie; rather there are no more Shakers to make pies, or there is one Shaker left who no longer makes pies. Will an Amish pie do?

Hey poem, you God's poem, what is happening today in Bloomfield? If you were God's poem you'd know. If you were really a true & perfect poem of God's, you'd know.

V

Dad is reading, I am reading.
Mom sleeps with the TV on.

A mammoth tooth larger than my hand turned up in a farmer's field.
Would I know it if it bit me?
I believe this tooth has been biting me all along. There are things that I wouldn't
know if they bit me: ghosts, truth, mammoth teeth.

Are we riding on the backs of mammoths unable to recognize them?
Are we trodding on the backs of something larger than ourselves?

Crickets sing.

Would it be easier to recognize Santa Claus or Jesus Christ if all you've ever
seen of them was pictures? I know both Santa & Christ equally, I have equal
collections of Santa & Christ knickknacks and both of them have bitten me.

I wish every day were a holiday and most of my days are of wine and tea roses.
What day is it Brenda? It's a holiday, I reply. Alternate parking rules apply.

So much reading and writing has already gone into this poem. This poem
wanted to imitate a piece of smart and beautiful writing. This poet wanted to
write a piece of writing.

An insect I recognize is biting me.

Each book an organ of thought, each book a brain sandwich. I thought of giving up the book (writings). One's head can't be filled with anything other than said book, thus making one look bookish.

What region of the brain do I use to think about you? You took me out of my headbook to answer. My ancestors are reading and sleeping in their graves. Now they dream.

I said a yard must be abundant in these things: a flying jenny, car bodies, lilies, camper shells, rabbits, plastic swimming pools take up all the space under the apple tree where the three-seater used to be. I stood looking down 3 holes empty, could see grasses and light coming through.

In first grade I prayed for God to send me a friend. It took almost a year to receive a friend from God.

Cricket, rub your back legs.

I've stopped writing, but keep reading, Reader. Open your vessel and keep reading.

We built a fire and roasted corn, tried to sleep under stars until I got scared of the night sky & the howling of dogs, didn't know they ruled the world after dark. I was in their territory and I was afraid, my best dog-friend I could no longer trust. In the sky I saw odd lights moving against all reason and us saying, what is that in the sky. All the other humans were in houses locked tight against us and the other animals. We knew better, not to know and knowing that while others are impatient, we can wait for Armageddon.

OTHER TITLES OF INTEREST BY COFFEE HOUSE PRESS

Easter Sunday by Tom Clark

Comrade Past and Mister Present by Andrei Codrescu

Maraca: New and Selected Poems 1965–2000 by Victor Hernández Cruz

Routine Disruptions by Kenward Elmslie

The Cloud of Knowable Things by Elaine Equi

Notes on the Possibilities and Attractions of Existence:
Selected Poems 1965–2000 by Anselm Hollo

Cranial Guitar by Bob Kaufman

Gorgeous Chaos: New and Selected Poems 1965–2001 by Jack Marshall

You Never Know by Ron Padgett

Of Flesh and Spirit by Wang Ping

Earliest Worlds by Eleni Sikelianos

Transcircularities: New and Selected Poems by Quincy Troupe

Breakers by Paul Violi

Helping the Dreamer: New and Selected Poems 1966–1988 by Anne Waldman

The Annotated "Here" and Selected Poems by Marjorie Welish

Available at fine bookstores everywhere.

Coffee House Press is a nonprofit literary publisher
supported in part by the generosity of readers like you.
We hope the spirit of our books makes you seek out
and enjoy additional titles on our list.
For information on how you can help bring
great literature onto the page,
visit coffeehousepress.org.

Funder Acknowledgments

Coffee House Press is an independent nonprofit literary publisher. Our books are made possible through the generous support of grants and gifts from many foundations, corporate giving programs, individuals, and through state and federal support. This reprint has received special project support from the Archie D. and Bertha H. Walker Foundation. The original publication of this book received major funding from the Jerome Foundation, and the National Endowment for the Arts, a federal agency. Coffee House Press receives major general operating support from the McKnight Foundation; from Target; and from the Minnesota State Arts Board, through an appropriation by the Minnesota State Legislature and from the National Endowment for the Arts, a federal agency. Coffee House also receives support from: an anonymous donor; the Elmer and Eleanor Andersen Foundation; the Buuck Family Foundation; the Patrick and Aimee Butler Family Foundation; Jennifer Haugh; Stephen and Isabel Keating; Allan and Cinda Kornblum; Mary McDermid; Stu Wilson and Melissa Barker; the Lenfestey Family Foundation; Rebecca Rand; Charles Steffey and Suzannah Martin; the law firm of Schwegman, Lundberg, Woessner, P.A.; the James R. Thorpe Foundation; the Woessner Freeman Family Foundation; and many other generous individual donors.

This activity is made possible in part by a grant from the Minnesota State Arts Board, through an appropriation by the Minnesota State Legislature and a grant from the National Endowment for the Arts.

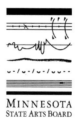

MINNESOTA
STATE ARTS BOARD

NATIONAL
ENDOWMENT
FOR THE ARTS

To you and our many readers across the country,
we send our thanks for your continuing support.

Good books are brewing at coffeehousepress.org